CONTENTS

HUMAN LIFE
AND
PROBLEMS

K. Sri Dhammananda

Publication of the

Buddhist Missionary Society
Buddhist Maha Vihara,
123, Jalan Berhala,
50470 Kuala Lumpur, Malaysia

Malaysian First Edition 1997
© 1997 by the author
All rights reserved

Perpustakaan Negara Malaysia
Cataloguing-in-Publication Data
Dhammananda, K. Sri., 1919-
Human Life and Problems
- K. Sri Dhammananda.
1st Edition
ISBN: 967-9920-73-9
1. Man (Buddhism).
2. Buddhism - Customs and Practices
3. Buddhism -Doctrines. 4. Man (Theology).
Buddhist Missionary Society
I . Title
294.3422

First printing: 15,000 copies (March 1997)
Lithography & Typeset by
Far East Offset & Engraving Sdn. Bhd.

Reprinted for free distribution by
The Corporate Body of the Buddha Educational Foundation
11F., 55 Hang Chow South Road Sec 1, Taipei, Taiwan, R.O.C.
Tel: 886-2-23951198 , Fax: 886-2-23913415

ABOUT THIS BOOK

The human brain that evolved far beyond the instinctive responses of other animals enabled man to create for himself a complex system whereby he commands an exalted position in the Universe. Man's position is relatively high, however insignificant he is in the Universe in respect of numbers. It is an accepted fact that 'what man conceives and believes, man can achieve.'

Birth as a man is a consequence of great meritorious actions in a past life. By virtue of being born as a man, he has the unique opportunity of consciously struggling to overcome evil and reach perfection. Earthly life as a human in fact is so important that all Buddhas elect to be born here for their final struggle and Enlightenment.

But man is beset with problems — human problems, of his own making, which tend to retard his progress in life. The impetus for writing this book arose from the urgent need to meet the many requests from concerned parents and citizens in view of the growing problems of juvenile delinquency, drug addiction among youths, sexual exploitation of children and a host of other immoral activities now plaguing all over the world. Many of these problems stem from lack of proper parental supervision at home as well as lack of moral upbringing through adherence to one's own religion. Many in fact treat their religion like a spare tyre – they never use it except in an emergency!

This book endeavours to portray these human problems analytically and present them with the Buddhist point of view through Buddhist approach and understanding.

As could be expected, the author was somewhat apprehensive at the beginning about undertaking a venture of this nature which can easily be quite controversial particularly when it comes to answering questions pertaining to certain areas of human problems like marital discords, divorce, homosexuality and the like which might be raised by certain quarters when seeking clarification. Hence, in writing a book of this nature the author inevitably had to traverse a veritable minefield with utmost care.

However he has had the benefit of assistance from several persons who were knowledgeable in these subjects and they generously gave him their expert advice in their respective areas of specialisation. They assisted him judiciously through such minefields of possible controversy. They also contributed valuable and constructive criticisms, comments and offered sound advice through various stages of his draft of this book.

To write a comprehensive book of this nature requires patience, diligence and devotion, all of which the author has displayed in a commendable manner. He has dealt with the various subjects as exhaustively as possible with a style which is both vigorous and candid.

One of his previous publications *'Why Worry'* in which he discussed several aspect of human problems with parables, was a well received book in many parts of the world and has even been translated into twelve other languages. We believe that this publication too will be beneficial to readers to understand fully the cause of many problems that we are confronted with today.

H.M.A. de Silva

14th March 1997.

ACKNOWLEDGEMENT

It is with great pleasure and gratitude that we acknowledge the selfless and invaluable services of the following persons who gave their full support and assistance in compilation of this book :–

Messers. H.M.A. de Silva, Vijaya Samarawickrama, Ven. Dhammawuddho, Eng Kwan Hai, Vincent Tsen Nyuk Vun, Quah Swee Kheng, Eddy Yu Chen Lim, Daphne Cheok, Tan Sor Huah, Kok Cheng Sim, Wong Su Leng, Sujatha Lim and Sister Subodhi for proof reading and also to Chong Hong Choo for supervision of the entire project, layout and design of the book cover.

HUMAN LIFE AND PROBLEMS

As human beings we have achieved a level of material progress we would not have even dreamed of barely a century ago. The marvels of modern technology have given us enormous power over the forces of nature. We have conquered many disasters but the ultimate question is: 'Are we happier than our ancestors were in the past?' The answer is 'No'.

The abuse of women, children and the underprivileged, religious and racial discrimination, colour bar and caste distinction continue on unabated.

Perhaps those who enjoy material comforts suffer even more acutely than their 'poor' fellow beings. Mental illnesses, stress and loneliness are some of the serious problems we now face in our modern society. But the vital question is: 'Who is responsible for all the evils that haunt the world today?'

There are many who are quite eager to take the credit for the progress that mankind has achieved. Religionists, scientists, politicians and economists — are all quick to claim that humanity is indebted to them for progress. But who must share the blame? I believe that everyone is equally responsible. Let us turn the spotlight on ourselves and ask ourselves to declare in all honesty if we also have been responsible for failing to bring peace and happiness to our fellow beings.

All of us are responsible for some of the horrors taking place in our midst today because we are too afraid to tell the truth. Let us take for example the exploitation of man's desire for sensual gratification. Greed for money and power has led some unscrupulous people to develop a multi-million dollar industry, to providing sensual pleasures in every possible way and young children are being trapped and victimized in the process.

Never before in the history of the world, has the human race been in such great need to be free from conflict, ill-feeling, selfishness, deceit and strife. We are in dire need of peace not only in our personal life at home and work, but also at the global level. The tension, anxiety and fear arising from the conflict are not only disruptive but continue to exert a constant drain on our well-being, mentally and physically. In their desire to completely dominate everything around them, humans have become the most violent beings in this world. They have succeeded, to some extent, but in so doing have paid a terrible price. They have sacrificed peace of mind for material comfort and power.

The basic problem we face today is moral degeneration and misused intelligence.

In spite of all the advances made by science and technology, the world is far from being safe and peaceful. Science and technology have indeed made human life more insecure than ever before. If there is no spiritual improvement in the way we handle our problems then humanity itself is in danger of being wiped out.

GOING BEYOND WORLDLY PLEASURES

The religions of the world have always maintained that human happiness does not depend merely upon the satisfaction of physical appetites and passions, or upon the acquisition of material wealth and power. Even if we have all the worldly pleasures, we still cannot be happy and peaceful if our minds are constantly obsessed with anxiety and hatred arising from ignorance with regard to the true nature of existence.

Genuine happiness cannot be defined solely in terms of wealth, power, children, fame or inventions. These no doubt bring some temporary physical and mental comfort but they cannot provide lasting happiness in the ultimate sense. This is particularly true when possessions are unjustly acquired or obtained through misappropriation. They become a source of pain, guilt and sorrow rather than bring happiness to the possessor.

Too often we are made to believe that pleasing the five senses can guarantee happiness. Fascinating sights, enchanting music, fragrant scents, delicious tastes and enticing body contacts mislead and deceive us, only to make us slaves to worldly pleasure. While no one will deny that there is momentary happiness in the anticipation of pleasure as well as during the gratification of the senses, such pleasures are fleeting. When one views these pleasures objectively, one will truly understand the fleeting and unsatisfactory nature of such pleasures. One will thus gain a better understanding of reality: what this existence really means and how true happiness can be gained!

We can develop and maintain inner peace only by turning our thoughts inwards instead of outwards. We must be aware of the dangers and pitfalls of the destructive forces of greed, hatred and delusion. We must learn to cultivate and sustain the benevolent forces of kindness, love and harmony. The battle-ground is within us and is not fought with weapons or with any other sources but only with our mental awarenes of all the negative and positive forces within our minds.

Mindfulness makes a full man. A full man speaks with an open mind. And like a parachute, the mind works better when it is fully opened. This awareness is the key to unlock the door from which conflict and strife as well as wholesome thoughts emerge.

The mind is the ultimate source of all happiness and misery. For there to be happiness in the world, the mind of an individual must first be at peace and happy. Individual happiness is conducive to the happiness of society, while the happiness of society means happiness of the nation. It is on the happiness of nations that the happiness of this world is built. Here we must use the image of a net. Imagine the whole universe as an immense net and each being as a single knot in this net. If we disturb one knot, the whole net is shaken. So each individual must be happy to keep the world happy.

From the lessons of life, it is clear that real victory is never gained by strife. Success is never achieved by conflict. Happiness is never experienced through ill-feeling. Peace is never achieved by accumulating more wealth or gaining worldly power. Peace is gained only by letting go of our selfishness and helping the world with acts of love. Peace in the heart conquers all opposing forces. It also helps us maintain a healthy mind and live a rich and fulfilling life of happiness and contentment. 'Since it is in the minds of men that wars are fought it is in the minds of men that the fortresses of peace must be built.

Sensual Pleasures

Today, especially in many so-called affluent societies, people are facing more problems, dissatisfaction and mental derangement than in under-developed societies. This is because men have become slaves to their sensual pleasures and crave for worldly enjoyment without proper moral and spiritual development. Their tensions, fears, anxieties and insecurity disturb their minds. This state of affairs has become the biggest problem in many countries. Since people in developed societies have not learnt to maintain contentment in their lives hence naturally they will experience unsatisfactoriness.

There are four areas where man is trying to find out the aim of life.

- Material or physical level;
- Likes and dislikes or pleasant and unpleasant feeling;
- Studying and reasoning;
- Sympathetic understanding, based on pure justice and fair dealing.

The last one is the realistic and lasting method which never creates disapointment. Today, people need more wealth, not only for their living and to fulfil their obligations, but because their craving for accumulation has increased. It has become a sort of competition.

To experience worldly pleasure there must be an external object or partner but to gain mental happiness it is not necessary to such have an external object.

Many young people have lost confidence in themselves and have to face difficulty in deciding what to do with their lives. The main cause of this mental attitude is excessive ambition and anxieties created by competition, jealousy and insecurity. Such problems naturally create a very bad atmosphere for others who want to live peacefully. It is a fact that when one individual creates a problem, his behaviour in turn affects the well-being of others.

Animals never experience happiness but pleasure. Happiness is not based on the arbitrary satisfaction of one's own self but in the sacrifice of one's pleasure for the well-being of others.

Using Wealth Properly

To most people a wealthy person, community or nation is one that is 'rich' in the sense of possessing assets or money which constitute material gain. The word 'wealth' originally meant state of well-being (weal). The word 'commonwealth' carries this meaning. But it is now used to refer to property which generally promotes material well-being, rather than the mental state of being well.

Of course we cannot deny that desire for wealth is a valuable adjunct to success if held within proper bounds. Desire, in itself, is not evil. Unrestrained, however, desire leads to restless discontentment, envy, greed, fear and cruelty to fellow beings. The accumulation of money may aid in the achievement of a kind of happiness to some extent, but does not in itself bring total satisfaction. Where most men of vast means fail is when they confuse the means with the end. They do not understand the nature, meaning and proper function of wealth, that it is merely a 'means' by which one can gain the 'end' of supreme happiness. But one can be happy without being rich. An old Chinese tale will illustrate this.

Once there was a king who wanted to know how to be truly happy. One of his ministers advised him that to be happy he would have to wear the shirt of a man who was truly happy. After a long time he found such a man, but the happy man had no shirt to give the king. That was why he was happy!

Wealth should be used well and wisely. It should be used for one's welfare as well as that of others. If a person spends his time clinging to his property, without fulfilling his obligations towards his country, people and religion, he will lead an empty life plagued with worries. Too many people are obsessed with material gain, to the point that they forget their responsibilities to their families and fellow beings. Happiness is a strange thing. The more you share it, the more you get satisfaction.

If one is selfish, when the time comes for one to leave this world, one will realise too late that one had not made full use of his or her wealth. No one, even a wealthy person, will have really benefited from the riches so painstakingly accumulated.

Accumulation of Wealth

Some people think that by accumulating more and more wealth, they can overcome their problems. So they try to become very rich by working hard, but after becoming billionaires, they have to face many more unexpected problems — insecurity, unrest, enemies and difficulty in maintaining their wealth. This, clearly shows that the accumulation of wealth alone is not the solution for human problems. Wealth no doubt can help to overcome certain problems but not all the world's happiness can be gained through money. Money cannot eradicate natural problems.

Philosophers, great thinkers and rationalists have pointed out the nature of human weaknesses and how to overcome them. However, many people regard them as mere theories and not as solutions to their problems. Sometimes the intellect actually creates more problems because it increases our egoistic opinions about ourselves.

The Buddha's Advice for Earning

Contrary to some misconceptions held by certain quarters that Buddhism, with its spirit of tolerance, and particularly in its practice of meditation, does not encourage its followers to work hard and to be industrious. The Buddha, in his many discourses, in fact strongly encouraged his followers not to be idle and indolent but to work hard and to be industrious so as to accumulate wealth through righteous means to maintain economic stability. Whilst encouraging the accumulation of wealth, the Buddha incidentally warned his followers not to violate any ethical or religious principles in so doing. He also advised that man should not become a slave to the mere accumulation of wealth just for accumulations sake but to protect it without neglect and waste. He advised that wealth should serve as an adequate means of livelihood for the family, should be utilised to assist relatives and friends where necessary, and to help the poor and needy as charitable acts.

In His discourse on various types of happiness in relation to wealth, the Buddha gave four practical classifications of happiness as follows:

- Happiness in the possession of wealth through righteous and legitimate means;
- Happiness through the proper and correct usage of accumulated wealth;
- Happiness in being free from indebtedness to anyone;
- Happiness in the knowledge that no illicit or illegitimate means had been employed in the course of accumulating wealth and that no one had been harmed or injured in so doing.

MAN'S PLACE ON THIS PLANET

From the Buddhist point of view, man is different from animals because only he alone has developed his intelligence and understanding to reflect his reasoning. Man means 'one who has a mind to think'. The purpose of religion is to help man to think correctly, to raise him above the level of the animal, to help him understand his relationship with his universe and live in harmony with it so that he reaches his ultimate goal of supreme happiness and fulfilment.

The three questions which have baffled man ever since he was able to satisfy his three basic survival needs of food, shelter and procreation are: 'Who am I? What am I doing here? Am I needed?' Throughout the history of man, many thought-systems have evolved, with religion being foremost among them, to provide answers to these questions. Naturally, since man asked them in the first place, the answers were all seen from the point of view of man himself.

Man in the Universe

Long ago man had seen himself as being in the centre of the Universe, as its most important inhabitant. According to this point of view, the world was made for humans, for themselves to obtain from it what they wanted because they were the most favoured creatures on it and everything that existed on this planet was for their sole pleasure.

This so called 'Humanistic' view may be directly responsible for the terrible rape of our planet and our total disregard for the rights of other beings which co-exist with us. For example, there have been tragic cases where certain species of animals became extinct through needless slaughter by unsympathetic humans in pursuit of their sporting pleasure or business purposes. Even today the subjugation of nature by science and technology is being applauded. We must increase the number of those amongst us who have already realised the vast destruction that has been wrecked by man in the name of 'progress'. Up until now nature has been most forgiving and it has allowed man to continue to think that this planet was made for him to rape and plunder at will, to satisfy his insatiable greed for material possessions and sensual gratification. Today there are many warning signs to indicate that the comfortable times are about to end. Hopefully, if Compassion and Right View will not save the world, then at least the same selfishness and desire for self-preservation and self-gratification will force man to give some sensible thought to our impoverished environment and our suffering fellow-creatures on this earth.

To understand the place of man in the Universe from a Buddhist point of view we must first of all look at the Buddha's views on the cosmos. According to him, the Universe is to be understood in terms of a vast cosmic space. His teaching categorised the whole universe into three groups: planets with living beings, planets with elements and only space itself.

We can see man as a specially favoured creature that had come into existence to enjoy the pleasures of a specially formed planet at the centre of the universe. Buddhism views man as a tiny being not only in strength but also in life span. Man is no more than just another creature but with intelligence that inhabits the universe.

Biologically, humans are weaker than any other beings big or small. Other animals are born armed with some sort of weapon for their own protection and survival. Humans, on the other hand have their mind for everything but not as a weapon. Humans are regarded as cultured living beings because they are to harmonise with others but not to destroy them. Religion was discovered by them for this purpose. Everything that lives share the same life force which energizes man. They are part of the same cosmic energy which takes various forms during endless rebirths, passing from human to animal, to divine form and back again, motivated by the powerful craving for existence (the survival instinct) which takes them from birth to death and to rebirth again in a never-ending cycle called *samsara*. The three detrimental sources of man which bind him to *samsara* are Greed, Hatred and Delusion.

This cycle can only be broken irrevocably through the development of Wisdom which destroy these fetters and puts an end to craving. Our shared fate as beings who inhabit this planet is that we all want desperately to go on living.

> 'All tremble at the rod
> All fear death
> Knowing this
> One should neither strike
> Nor cause to strike'   ~ Dhammapada

All things depend on each other for their existence. A man cannot see himself as different from (let alone being superior to) other beings because his body is solely dependent on food, which means he is dependent on plants, water, oxygen, etc. for his existence. At the same time his mind also exists dependently because the existence of thoughts rely on sense data which are derived from the external world of objects and persons. The whole universe must be seen as an immense net: if only one knot in it is shaken, the whole net vibrates. Man owes allegiance to the world because he is dependent on it for his existence both physically and mentally. His attitude towards the world should therefore not be the arrogance of a pampered only child but one of humility: the world was not made for him alone, nor is the world always made out in his favour. Worldly conditions have no favouritism; they are neither kind nor cruel but neutral. Man exists because the rest of the world allows him to do so.

Therefore he should not try to squeeze things out from the world only for his own benefit. He must maintain a sense of awe and respect towards nature and all beings. Man is a relative newcomer to the planet Earth. He must learn to respect his other brethren. He must learn to behave more like a guest rather than a player in a card game where the winner takes all.

It was in recognition of this interdependence that the Buddha advised his followers to practise *metta* (loving-kindness) to all, to radiate that compassion towards all beings. The Buddha does not mean that men should extend their love to fellow human beings only (he certainly does not recommend special treatment for their 'fellow Buddhists'). Whenever he talks about loving others he always speaks of 'all beings' (*sabbe satta*) even those lacking material form, the conscious, the super conscious.

Three modes of birth: living beings are those that are moisture-born, egg-born, womb-born and those spontaneously arising in other planes of existence. Clearly the Buddha was teaching that if a man is to live on this planet he must develop an attitude of loving kindness towards not only fellow human beings but all beings that inhabit this planet as well as in other planes of existence. Only then can he vanquish the selfish thoughts which place his needs and survival above the needs of all others.

In Buddhist cosmology man is simply the inhabitant of one of the existing planes one can go to after death. These range from superconscious levels through the high ly sensuous down to the four unhappy states. Man occupies a mid-way position in these realms. The so-called divine realms are 'happy' state but they too are impermanent. Although there are indications to lead us to believe that some intelligent living beings do exist in other world systems, it is not verifiable whether there are beings similar to humans in other planets of the universe. It is in terms of this infinite vast cosmic context that Buddhism tries to understand the place of man in the universe. In terms of that context man seems to be small. We must add to this man's propensity for cruelty, for his ability to inflict pain on others which makes him at times far less admirable than animals which only attack to satisfy their basic need for food, shelter or sex.

Man's Unique Position

One might argue that this is a very negative view of man, relegating him to an inferior position and disregarding his magnificent achievements in philosophy, religion, psychology, science, the arts, architecture, literature and development of culture and the like. Far from it; in this cosmic context humans assume a unique position because they have the most rare privilege of easy accessibility to salvation. It is for three reasons.

Human world is a good, well-balanced mixture of pleasure and pain. When pleasure is intensified (in the divine realms) or pain is predominant (in the lower worlds) one's mind does not turn towards spirituality. Buddhists maintain that extreme austerity or extreme self indulgence are not conducive to the development of wisdom and understanding. The Middle Path between extreme pleasure and austerity is advocated and the human world provides man the opportunity to tread the Middle Path. The second reason is the relative short span of human life and the unpredictability of the time of death. Faced with imminent death one is more often inclined towards spirituality. The third reason is that while in other realms the inhabitants are mere passive recipients of the effects of their past *kamma*, man is in a favourable position to create fresh *kamma*, and is thus able to shape his own destiny.

All of this gives man the responsibility to work out his own salvation in the human plane. He is in effect his own Creator and Saviour. Many others believe that religion has come down from heaven but Buddhists know that Buddhism started on the earth and reached heaven.

What this implies is that each man has within him the Buddha-seed (potential for perfection) which he can develop without any external aid. One can become a Buddha through birth in the human plane, because it is here that he can experience existence in its entirety. Buddhists would certainly agree with Shakespeare's view of the human paradox:-

What a piece of work is man,
how noble in reason,
how infinite in faculties in form
  and moving;
how express and admirable in action,
how like an angel in apprehension,
how like a god: the beauty of the world,
  the paragon of animals;
and yet to me what is this quintessence
  of dust?

                                        ~Hamlet 2:2

In many ways man is ignorant, yet he has the seed to become the highest of all beings: a fully enlightened one. Some people say that human life is between heaven and hell because the human mind can be developed easily to experience heavenly bliss, and when it is abused it could very easily experience suffering in hell.

Man is man only if he has that human concern or human heartedness

Proud man hath no heaven;
The envious man hath no neighbour;
An angry man hath not even himself.
                          -Chinese philosophy

'The individual by himself is helpless. Hence the social life of man which brings forth co-operative power. Man cannot be man without society. Man is one with nature.' (Greek philosopher).

In the teaching of the Buddha it is mentioned that human beings experience heavenly bliss when the objects impinging on the five senses are favourable and soothing.

On the other hand they also experience suffering like in hell if the objects are irritable and disturbing.

What Buddhism requires of Man

What does Buddhism require of man? A Chinese scholar once asked a monk what constituted the essence of Buddhism and the sage replied: –

> *To do good, not to do evil*
> *To purify the mind,*
> *This is the teaching of all the Buddhas.*

Naturally this scholar had expected a much more 'profound' answer, something deep and abstruse, and he remarked that even a child of three could understand that. But the sage replied that while a child of three could understand it, a man of eighty could not practise it!

The Buddha had similarly cautioned his attendant disciple, Ananda not to regard seemingly simple teachings as something easy to follow.

This is the essence of Buddhism — Man is required to follow startlingly 'simple' precepts in his search for emancipation, but the practice of these can be extremely difficult. To begin with:

- he must not take the life of any living creature knowingly;
- he must not take anything not given;

- he must refrain from lying and harsh frivolous speech;
- he must guard against sexual misdemeanour;
- he must not take anything (like drugs and liquor) which causes him to lose his mind fulness.

These are important Buddhist principles to observe.

These principles are not meant for expression but to be simply put into practice with understanding. The central problem of the spiritual life is one of active, practical application, not a matter of intellectual knowledge.

The ultimate aim of man in Buddhism is to break finally and irrevocably the bonds that bind him to constant rebirth in the repeated birth – and – death cycle of *samsara*. He is destined to be subjected to an endless round of rebirths because in his ignorance, man conceives of an enduring entity called an 'ego' or 'self '.

Taking the illusion of an ego for real he develops selfish desires. Man is thus endlessly struggling to satisfy his cravings but he is never satisfied. It is like scratching a sore to find temporary relief, only to discover that in doing so the itch has increased because the sore has been aggravated.

THE INSTITUTION OF MARRIAGE

Marriage is a partnership in which two individuals of opposite sexes but equal worth as human beings choose to live together. A happy and lasting marriage requires a lot of hard work and commitment where love is fed with shared experiences, joys and sorrows.

Marriage is the culmination of love by two individuals committed to one another by a common bond. 'How do I love thee? Let me count the ways. I love thee to the depth and breadth and height my soul can reach. ... ' (Robert Browning). We believe as Browning does, that love is the essence of life itself, something which transcends boundaries, race and creed.

Marriage has failed to fulfil its purposes today because people have failed to recognize the importance of equality and respect for women. These privileges are enjoyed by many women in a large number of areas of human activity. Strangely when it comes to marriage, women are still treated badly. The importance of the role of women in society was undoubtedly widened after the advent of Buddhism in India, giving them a wide scope to venture into vocations besides house-keeping. In spite of this, for the vast majority, to get married and rear children remained the normal choice of career.

But there was a difference; married life was ennobled by the noble position given to it by the Buddha himself to such an undertaking. He lifted the married woman from a state of servant to a state of responsibility and importance. As an indication of the Buddha's concern for maintenance of happiness through marriage, he laid down specific instructions for the guidance of husband and wife.

The Buddha was full of praise for happy couples. Among his lay disciples were Nakulamata and Nakulapita who were considered most eminent for having lived together amicably for a long time. The Buddha praised them and gave instructions to others as to how they too could live happily in marriage. These instructions given over two thousand five hundred years ago hold good even to this day. Much misery has been experienced in modern times by men and women in married life because they deviated from these instructions.

The institution of marriage in ancient India was governed by the concept of caste, the position of women, the rights of men and the four stages of the individual's life. The Buddha's rejection of the concept of the caste system meant that the Buddhist institution of marriage was emancipated from these rigid and inflexible rules, regulations and rituals which had become a great obstacle to the free and unprejudiced behaviour of the members of society, both male and female.

The discourse on Fundamentals of Buddhist Social Ethics, *(Sigalovada Sutta)* generally lays down the basic pattern of relationships between husband and wife, parents and children, and enumerates the reciprocal duties that bind them together emphasising the most essential aspects of their common life.

The comprehensive study of the Buddhist institution of marriage outlined in the Buddha's teaching clearly shows that was intended for the enjoyment, promotion and moralization of biological needs, psycho-logical satisfaction and material well-being of both husband and wife without any reference to specific customs, sacraments or any kind of ideology, religious or otherwise.

According to the Buddha, cultural compatibility between husband and wife was considered as one of the factors of a successful married life. Many of today's problems in marriage arise from the inability of the parties concerned to recognize the sacrifices involved. Marriage is not simply lust and romance. Romance is not a bad thing in itself, but it is emotional and has limitations.

There will be less disillusion and heartache in marriage if we understand that, from the illusions of romance, a deep and abiding love may emerge. Love is a passionate and abiding desire, on the part of two people, to produce together conditions under which each can express his or her real self and to produce together an intellectual soil and an emotional climate in which each can flourish, far superior to what either could achieve alone.

In the past we heard of blissfully married couples who shared the sweetness of love earned through years of being together, for better or for worse. For most who have been long-married couples, 'happily ever after' did not just happen. Couples in long, happy marriages mentioned this fact of life when asked what made their relationships a success. 'We worked to keep the romance alive. We enjoyed our differences and learned from them.

'We voiced our discontents freely and dealt with them right away instead of letting them build into thunderclouds'. But in a way, the thing all successful couples have in common was reflected in this observation: 'Even when things were really bad, we were both too stubborn to quit'. Perhaps what characterizes modern couples with problems is that they want things to work out too easily as it happens on television. No, everything good must be earned through hard work.

For many the road to marital longevity has not been smooth. The bumps included many things: inability to have children, the death of a child, a disabled child, a difficult economic crisis and highly stressful career changes.

Although none of the couples surveyed said so specifically, it was obvious that two other factors were important to their marital success. Firstly, even though some couples faced considerable differences in personality and sometimes carried heavy emotional baggage, they maintained respect for one another always and refrained from trying to remake their partners. A wife once told her husband 'You married me for what I am.' He retorted, 'No, I married you for what you would become.' Now of course both parties were wrong because their expectations were different and they were unwilling to compromise. Secondly, none of the marriages was marred by psychological disturbances too severe to preclude a true partnership. There was a wife who always used to insult her husband even for a minor mistake stating: 'You are a stupid man.' The husband on the other hand was a very tolerant man. However, one day when he was scolded by the wife using the same word the husband retorted: 'I think you are right. If I were not a stupid man, do you think that I would ever marry a woman like you?' From that day onwards she did not repeat that insulting word.

To achieve a successful marriage, couples also need to understand and accept the differences between the two genders. Couples sometimes become frustrated with each other and wish that their partner was more like them. Knowing and being able to tolerate the differences between men and women helps a lot in marriage.

A mate who is willing to weather the hard times and make the adjustments that come with children, job changes, financial difficulties or simply learning more about the person one is married to is the real secret to a successful marriage.

Another saying on married life: 'Wife becomes a mistress to a young man, a companion to the middle aged and a nurse to an old man.'

Many couples with children are determined to stay together at least until their children are grown up. With just a little effort these years can be among the most fulfilling times in a marriage.

Marriage is a blessing but many people turn their married lives into misery and a curse. Poverty is not the main cause of an unhappy married life. Both husband and wife must learn to share the pleasure and pain of everything in their daily lives. Mutual understanding is the secret of a happy family life.

In a true marriage, man and woman think more of the partnership than they do of themselves individually. Marriage is a bicycle made for two. A feeling of security and contentment comes from mutual efforts.

A wife is not her husband's servant. She deserves respect as an equal. Though a man is generally regarded even today as being the bread winner helping out with household chores do not demean his masculinity. At the same time, a nagging and grumpy wife is not going to make up for shortages in the home. Neither will her suspicion of her husband help to make a happy marriage. If her husband has shortcomings, only tolerance and kind words will get him to see light. It is important in marriage to keep tolerance alive throughout. Little things can mean a lot. Right understanding and moral conduct are the practical sides of wisdom.

From time immemorial, flowers have been considered the language of love. They don't cost much. Wives, or for that matter all women, attach a lot of importance to birthdays and anniversaries, and caring husbands should never be too busy to keep love alive with little tributes and attentions. Trivialities such as these are at the bottom of most marital happiness. Wives do appreciate such little attentions from their courteous husbands and it is this lifelong goodwill that keeps the home fires burning.

A carefully developed family affection is a simple formula that works both for keeping marriages together and bringing up children of good character. True love means being willing to value one's partner and being unwilling to devalue him or her in the presence of other people. This willingness has to spring from the heart. The key difference between marriages that work and those that do not is how much a couple value each other. Criticising, putting down or belittling a spouse particularly in the presence of other people, erodes a relationship. And even this is not enough as each still has to value the other as if he or she is a rare gem.

Sometimes words are not necessary if there is understanding. An elderly father once confessed to his children that he loved their mother very much and told them to take care of her always, even after he was no more. He confided to them that she was the best woman in the world and that the family was indeed lucky to have her around. The wife, now in her

60's, has seven grown children and as many grandchildren. Yet she confessed that she never once heard the endearing words 'I love you' ever uttered or whispered to her — not even a variation of it. The wife, who belongs to the old school of Chinese philosophy, is quite content with her husband's own caring ways and concern for her happiness in their blissful married life. Her female intuition somehow tells her that deep down in his heart he truly loves her and that she could not have been dealt a better deck of cards. It is in the nature of some people not to speak out their feelings, but they care. We have to watch out for their actions. The next key to a harmonious marriage is to work towards achieving one's objective. It is a law of nature that if no effort is put into, for instance, a garden, weeds will grow instead of beautiful flowers. The same goes for marriage.

Faith, not necessarily in the religious sense, (though it helps tremendously if a couple shares similar religious beliefs) is another vital ingredient in a lasting relationship.

How important is sex in a marriage? Sex is a natural instinct and if enjoyed within its proper boundaries can bring about great happiness. Sex helps to keep a marriage glowing, and is an important and vital area that keeps a marriage together. It creates intimacy, a shared experience between two people which no one else is party to. It makes the relationship precious, and private.

The important thing to appreciate here is the fact that men and women see sex differently. While men may view sex as an intense physical activity, women do not. For her, it involves an interaction with the man she loves, that is with his gentleness, his care and concern. Understanding the fact that women need intimacy and closeness makes the sexual activity a lot more meaningful and fulfilling.

Sex is much more than the gratification of an appetite. It is the basis of an intimate lifelong companionship, and the means of bringing into the world children whom we love and cherish as long as we live.

Through the ages we have learned that love and mutual respect must be the basis of close intimacy between the sexes. Sex, like any other tendency in man, must be regulated by reason. Man, not being governed by instincts like lesser animals, would find his tendencies running wild were he not to regulate them with reason.

There is a saying: 'Like fire, sex is a good servant but a bad master.'

A society grows through a network of

relationships which are mutually intertwined and inter-dependent. Every relationship is a wholehearted commitment to support and to protect others in a group or community.

Marriage plays a very important part in this strong web of relationships of giving support and protection. A good marriage should grow and develop gradually from understanding and not impulse, from true loyalty and not just sheer indulgence.

The institution of marriage provides a fine basis for the development of culture, a delightful association of two individuals to be nurtured, and to be free from loneliness, deprivation and fear. In marriage, each partner develops a complementary role, giving strength and moral courage to each other, with each manifesting a supportive and appreciative recognition to the other's skills.

There must be no thought of man or woman being superior — each is complementary to the other, a partnership of equality, exuding gentleness, generosity, calm and dedication and most important of all, self-sacrifice.

The Buddha's advice to a couple
•• The Wife

In advising women about their role in married life, the Buddha appreciated the fact that peace and harmony of a home rested largely on a woman. His advice was realistic and practical when he explained a number of day-to-day characteristics which a woman should or should not cultivate. On diverse occasions, the Buddha counselled that a wife should: –

- not harbour evil thoughts against her husband;
- not be cruel, harsh or domineering;
- not be spendthrift but should be economical and live within her means;
- guard and save her husband's hard-earned earnings and property;
- always be attentive and chaste in mind and action;
- be faithful and harbour no thought of any adulterous acts;
- be refined in speech and polite in action;
- be kind, industrious and hardworking;
- be thoughtful and compassionate towards her husband;
- be modest and respectful;
- be cool, calm and understanding – serving not only as a wife but also as a friend and adviser when the need arises.

According to Buddhist teaching, in a marriage, the husband can expect the following qualities from his wife: –

– love:

A deep and abiding love is the most emotional and spontaneous expression of desire and self-fulfilment a husband expects of his wife. It is indeed the basis of an intimate life-long mutual relationship and the means of bringing into the world children whom they will love and cherish as long as they live. Here love is not limited to mere attachment *(prema)*, but it is an all pervading quality of wishing for the genuine well-being of her husband.

– attentiveness:

To be ever heedful, mindful and diligent, as well as to give her undivided attention to her husband's needs;

– family obligations:

Besides fulfilling the duties and responsibilities of the couple's own family, the wife should also honour and respect her in-laws and deserving relatives and treat them as she would her own parents;

– faithfulness:

Is associated with chastity, fidelity and steadfastness of the wife. It also implies being trust worthy and giving her constant devotion to her husband;

– child-care:

Motherly love is the foundation of all love in the world. As a devoted mother she would, through her maternal instincts, even venture out at the risk of her life, for the protection of her only child;

– thrift:

As the wife is entrusted with the task of home management, it is incumbent on her to see that household expenditure is kept well within the family budget provided by the husband. To accomplish this task, the wife has to economise on her expenditure and exercise thrift, even to the extent of being frugal in doing so;

– the provision of meals:

As the mistress of the house, it is the duty of the wife to prepare good nourishing food for the family. The family meal is an important event each day as it develops goodwill and togetherness;

– to calm him down when he is upset:

When the husband returns home in an agitated state, the wife has to express herself in a soothing manner so as to pacify and comfort him. This will ease the situati;

– sweetness in everything:
Besides expressing her endearing and tender feelings, the wife should also possess a charming disposition, be always cheerful, pleasant and comely.

•• **The Husband**
The Buddha, in reply to a householder as to how a husband should minister to his wife, declared that the husband should always honour and respect his wife, by being faithful to her, by giving her the requisite authority to manage domestic affairs and by giving her befitting ornaments. This advice, given over twenty five centuries ago, still stands good till today.

Over the centuries, male dominated societies have perpetuated the myth that men are superior to women but the Buddha made a remarkable change and uplifted the status of woman by a simple suggestion that a husband should honour and respect his wife. Such a remark maybe common today, but when we consider it was made in India 2500 years ago, it is no less than revolutionary!

A husband should be faithful to his wife which means that a husband should fulfil and maintain his marital obligations to his wife, thus sustaining the confidence in the marital relationship in every sense of the word.

The husband, being the bread-winner, has to invariably be away from home, hence he should entrust the domestic or household duties to the wife who should be considered as the custodian and manager of their property and as the home economic-administrator.

The provision of befitting ornaments to the wife should be symbolic of the husband's love, care and appreciation showered on her. This symbolic practice has been carried out from time immemorial in Buddhist communities.

Unfortunately today it is in danger of dying out because of the adverse influence of the modern way of life.

The wife's expectations from the husband are: –

– tenderness:
Being gentle and respectful to the wife on all matters when attending to her needs:

– courtesy:
Being polite, obliging, civil and modest in his dealings and consultations with his wife:

– sociability:
Being genial, friendly, communicative and compatible at all times with his wife in the company of their friends and visitors to

their home;

– security:
The principal objective a wife seeks in her marriage is security to be provided by her husband.

In this respect the husband is expected to be a tower of strength so as to withstand any form of external threat to the family and to provide them with adequate protection and safety at all times;

– fairness:
As a responsible husband, he should be forgiving, compassionate and merciful as well as being charitable to deserving causes needing his assistance. As a father, he has to be just and reasonable to the demands of his growing children;

– loyalty:
As an understanding husband, he should give his undivided loyalty to his wife and stand by her, through thick and thin, under any adverse situation confronting the family.

He should be steadfast in his principles and one whom the wife could, with complete confidence, depend upon in facing any untoward eventuality;

– honesty:
Being a responsible husband, he has to be upright in his character and be frank with his wife on all matters affecting themselves and their children. He should not harbour any secrets from his wife as this will ultimately erode her trust and confidence in him;

– good companionship:
The husband should possess an amiable personality and be able to mix with people from all walks of life. He should be knowledgeable so as to be able to engage in intelligent conversation at all levels of society and be approachable to anyone needing his assistance. He also should possess a good sense of humour to enliven his listeners who seek his companionship; and

– moral support:
As a responsible husband, he should be able to stand steadfastly by his wife's side to the very end, in the face of any untoward eventuality confronting her and lend her moral support and much – needed courage to overcome such a situation.

•• Husband and Wife
The husband is the acknowledged head of the family, unless he is incapacitated from

performing his duties as such. Both in common law and under modern legislation, the husband is legally bound to support his wife and family, notwithstanding the fact that the wife has her own property or income or is capable of earning her own support.

Even today where many wives work, the nurturing of a family should be a shared experience. Husbands have no reason to shirk household duties, to help the wife and train the children, especially when there are no servants to do such work.

Apart from these emotional and sensual aspects, the couple will have to take care of day-to-day living conditions, family budget and social obligations.

Thus, mutual consulations between the husband and wife on all family problems would help to create an atmosphere of trust and understanding in resolving whatever issues that may arise.

The Five Duties to be performed by parents towards their children

According to the Buddha there are five duties that should be performed by parents toward their children.

- The first duty is to dissuade them from evil
Home is the first school, and parents are the

first teachers. Children usually take their elementary lessons on good and evil from their parents. Careless parents directly or indirectly impart an elementary knowledge of lying, cheating, dishonesty, slandering, revenge, shamelessness and fearlessness towards evil and immoral activities to their children during childhood. Remember the habit of aping.

Parents should therefore show exemplary conduct and should not transmit such vices into their children's impressionable minds.

– The second duty is to persuade them to be good
Parents are the teachers at home; teachers are the parents in school. Both parents and teachers are equally responsible for the future and well-being of the children, who become what they are made into. They are, and they will be, what the adults are. They sit at the feet of the adults during their impressionable age.

They imbibe what is imparted. They follow in their footsteps. They are influenced in thoughts, words and deeds. As such it is the duty of the parents to create the most congenial atmosphere both at home and in the school.

Simplicity, obedience, co-operation, unity, self-sacrifice, honesty, straightforwardness, service, self-reliance, contentment, good manners, religious zeal and other kindred virtues should be inculcated in their juvenile minds by degrees. Seeds so planted will eventually grow into fruit-laden trees.

– The third duty is to give the children a good education
A decent education is the best legacy that parents can bestow upon their children. A more valuable treasure there is not. It is the best blessing that parents could confer on their children.

Education should be imparted to them, preferably from youth, in a religious atmosphere by training them to uphold noble human disciplines and humane qualities. This has a far-reaching effect on their lives.

– The fourth duty is to see that they are married to suitable individuals
Marriage is a solemn act that pertains to one's whole lifetime; this union should be one that cannot be dissolved easily. Hence, marriage has to be viewed from every angle and in all its aspects to the satisfaction of all parties concerned before the wedding.

Parents' observations of their children's life partners is important for their future married life. While parents must accept modern practices like dating and so on, children must know clearly that parents have a right to monitor their activities, know who their friends are. But there must be also a right to privacy and self respect.

According to Buddhist culture, duty supersedes right. Let both parties be not adamant, but use their wise discretion and come to an amicable settlement.

Otherwise, there will be mutual cursing and other repercussions. More often than not the infection is transmitted to progeny as well. It is said that in most cases people who perpetrate abuse of others were themselves the victims of abuse.

– The last duty is to hand over to them, at the proper time, their inheritance
Parents not only love and tend their children as long as they are still in their custody, but also make preparations for their future comfort and happiness. They acquire treasures through personal discomfort and ungrudgingly give them as a legacy to their children.

Parents who bequeath their wealth do not want their children to squander it but to benefit from the inheritance so that it will enhance their living standard. In all of this the bottom line is mutual respect, and concern for the welfare of both parents and children.

Parental Responsibilities in the upbringing of their children

Parenting is not like any other 9 to 5 job. It is never ending and there is never enough time to do everything. No matter how old your baby is, newborn or toddler, it is never too late to put your baby first and enjoy being a mum or dad.

Many parents think that they alone know what is best for the children and therefore expect too much from them. They force their children into tuition classes even if they can cope with their studies. At the same time they are asked to take up ballet dancing (in the case of girls), taekwando (in the case of boys), music lessons, computer classes and so on. On top of this, they insist that their children obtain straight 'A's in their examinations and excel in everything else. In this rat-race they turn their children into display objects; possessions which they can be proud to show off to their friends and relatives and for others to talk about.

In the good old days life as a child and a teenager was never stressful because there were not too many expectations to fulfil. But children these days, especially those in urban areas, seem to have so many things to do and compete in that they are deprived of a normal childhood. Many people fail to realise that as parents, they have certain rights and also responsibilities. The child has his or her rights and responsibilities too. What we have today are people who want to be super parents, but in many cases the children do not turn out to be super. Parents should therefore be realistic and reasonable. They should not set targets which they well know their children cannot fulfil, thus avoiding unnecessary stress and disappointment to the family. Building a happy family is a continuous process.

Hence parents must not only be fully aware of their role and responsibilities, but also apply modern techniques in parenting accordingly. Remember the saying of the Taoist philosopher, Zhuang Zu; 'If you have 6 fingers do not try to make them 5, and if you have 5 fingers do not try to make them 6. Do not go against nature.'

You are responsible as a concerned parent for the well-being and up-bringing of your children. If the child grows up to be a strong, healthy and useful citizen, it is the result of your efforts. If the child grows up to be a delinquent, it is you who must bear the responsibility. Do not blame others. As parents, it is your bounden duty to guide your child on a proper path. Although there are a few incorrigible cases of juvenile delinquency, nevertheless as parents, you are morally responsible for the behaviour of your children.

Parental support and control have to be adjusted as the child grows. The ultimate goal of parenting is to become a friend to your child but only according to his capacity to accept responsibility. A mistake some parents make is that they want to be a friend to their six-year old. But we need to be careful about what we mean by friend. We certainly do not mean we treat a child as if he is an equal in maturity. But there must be love, trust and respect. At that age, a child needs a parent, not a friend. While building a loving and supportive relationship with the children, it is recommended that parents help them develop spiritually.

Above all you must have time for your child. Time to answer his questions, to help him understand the wonder of life. You have to bear in mind that you are stifling the creativity in your child when you do not answer the questions that he is raising. When a child is asking questions, he is indeed seeking to communicate, so the biggest challenge confronting you is to respond readily with love, and everything you do should be congruent with the natural inquisitiveness in a child.

Being spontaneous is also important in getting children involved in things and the greatest scientists have been known to be spontaneous. If parents do not know the answers to questions they must make it a point to find it out for their children instead of brushing them off and telling them that they are too busy, or it is not important, thus shutting them up and stifling their curiosity. You will feel guilty about telling your children during their most tender and inquisitive age: 'Don't ask so many questions!.' As a caring and responsible parent you should in fact respond readily to that natural inquisitiveness in your child.

The scientific way of solving a problem is to look at the problem, find all the data available and then put together a solution in a coherent manner. Likewise, a child whose curiosity meets with a favoured response will learn to think and act scientifically as well as creatively and it will serve him well into adulthood.

For instance, when you give a toy to your child, you should give it with tender love and joy. Instead, certain parents tend to almost shout: 'Don't open it like that. Don't break the toy, it is very expensive. Do you know how lucky you are to get such a toy?' So what if he indeed breaks the toy? If you can afford to buy the toy, he will quite logically think he can afford to break it.

You could instead be part of his discovery by telling him: 'Come my dear, let's open the toy box together,' and use the fun element instead of the negative element. Give the present with joy and love. It can be done if you are not stressed and unhappy yourself. You must be happy for it is only in a state of happiness that one is comfortable and generous.

Parents sometimes are to be blamed for unwittingly inculcating negative social habits in their children. For instance, a parent who asks a child to say that he or she is not in when answering a phone call (a seemingly innocent act) plants the first seed of falsehood in the tender mind of the young. If allowed to flourish in an environment not conducive to promoting human values, the child may well, in the future, become a destructive element to the peace, happiness and well being of family and society, and more importantly, to himself.

Many parents and elders are today responsible for planting these seeds of false-hood in many different ways. They either encourage falsehood directly, or by acting or speaking falsely, initiate and allow the vicious cycle of human value degradation to develop. The fate of our children may well depend upon the parents and elders developing a right attitude to moral upbringing truth and truthful living.

Children echo the language of their

parents. To prevent the use of rude or vulgar words, responsible parents should use pleasant terms, as children generally tend to imitate their parents.

A child at its most impressionable age needs the love, care, affection and attention of the parents. Without parental love and guidance, the child will be emotionally handicapped and will find the world a bewildering place to live in. Showering parental love on the other hand does not mean pandering to all the demands of the child, reasonable or otherwise. Too much pampering would in fact spoil the child. The mother in bestowing her love and care, should also be strict and firm, but not harsh, in handling the child. Show your love with a disciplined hand – the child will understand.

Parents should spend more quality time with their children, particularly during their formative years. They should consider giving their children the gift of healthy parenting instead of showering them with material presents. This gift includes building a child's self-esteem, striving for positive communication, granting unconditional love and eliminating aspects that hinder the child's psychological development. These are gifts with true, deeper meaning. Healthy parenting is the greatest gift a child can receive and a parent can give.

Unfortunately, amongst present-day parents, parental love is sadly lacking. The mad rush for material advancement, the liberation movements and the aspiration for equality among the sexes have all resulted in many mothers joining their husbands, spending their working hours in offices and shops, rather than remaining at home and tending to their off-spring. The children, left to the care of relations, day-care centres or paid servants, are bewildered on being denied tender motherly love and care.

Providing the child with all sorts of sophisticated modern toys (as a form of appeasement) such as tanks, machine guns, pistols, or swords that are detrimental to character formation is not psychologically advisable. Loading a child with such toys is no substitute for a mother's tender love and affection. The child as a result is unwittingly taught to condone aggression and destruction instead of being taught to be kind, compassionate and helpful. Such a child will develop brutal tendencies as it grows up. Devoid of parental affection and guidance, it will not be surprising if the child subsequently grows up to be a delinquent. Then, who is to be blamed for bringing up such a wayward child? The parents of course!

The working mother, especially after a hard day's work in an office, followed by household chores, can hardly find time for the child that is yearning for her care and attention. Parents who have no time for their children now should not complain later in life when these same children have no time for them. Parents who claim that they spend a lot of money on their children but are too busy should not complain when in later life their 'busy' children in turn decide to leave them in Homes for the Aged!

Most women work today so that the family can enjoy more material benefits. They should seriously consider Gandhi's advice for men to seek freedom from greed rather than freedom from need. Of course, given today's economic set-up we cannot deny that some mothers are forced to work. In such a case, the father and mother must make extra sacrifices of their time to compensate for what their children miss when they are away. If both parents spend their non-working hours at home with their children, there will be greater harmony and understanding between parents and children. We call this 'quality time'. with the family.

Children who are left in the care of relatives, day care centres or paid servants, as well as latch key children who are left to their own devices at home, are often deprived of motherly love and care. The mother, feeling guilty about this lack of attention, will try to placate the child by giving in to all sorts of demands. Such action only spoils the child.

Most men devote their energies and creativity to their work and thus what energy they have reserved for the family are merely the 'left overs'. Here is where the argument for quality time comes in, usually from guilty parents who want to justify whatever time they have left for their children. One of the flaws of the quality time concept lies in the fact that the needs of the children and the availability of the parents do not always converge. When the children need them, they are not around.

Parents are often placed in a dilemma. Rushing home from a hard day's work, weary parents have their own family chores waiting for them. When the day's work is done, it would be time for dinner followed by watching T.V., and whatever time there is left is hardly enough to attend to a child's rightful dues of parental love and affection. More importantly, parents are not around to transmit cultural, social and religious values to their children at times when children are best attuned to receive them. This cannot be done during 'quality time'!

Some working parents may even take their work home or even bring back the stress and tension they gathered from their work place. As a result, they may lose their tempers at the children.

As husband and wife they may not have enough time together and this may even lead to broken marriages. There should be increased awareness that strong family ties can contribute to the healthy growth of a child.

It can be said that gender differences do operate in parent/child relationships. It is said that mothers and their grown-up daughters communicate more often, even after the daughters are married and have left home.

On the other hand, it is different for fathers and grown-up sons. They are said to only speak when absolutely necessary and often about nothing serious. The conversation can be like a question and answer session.

The father perhaps thinks the son is a big boy and that he should know his role and duties at home, towards his parents and outside. But with mothers, it is different — the daughter is forever 'my little girl.'

Whatever it is, parents have an important role to play in bringing up their children and doing it well if they want to help ease the many ills plaguing our society today. Good values cannot be taught through words, but through deeds.

Parents must be good models themselves. The old parental attitude that 'you do whatever father tells you to do and not what he does,' does not hold water any more. Parents must be of the right character themselves. If we want our children to begin life well, with the proper values, we have to start at home.

If things aren't good between the boys and their fathers, the latter must begin to look for answers within themselves.

Sacrifices by both parents are needed. They should make time and try as far as possible to get the family members involved in all activities pursued, by creating family – oriented activities.

The essence is on setting their priorities right e.g. a priority oriented towards the family and marriage, thus creating a close-knit family relationship for a harmonious environment.

A Happy Family

It is true in every society that a family is the smallest social unit. If every family in a country is happy, the whole nation will be happy. What constitutes a happy family? A happy family is defined as one that is stable in terms of social, economic, psychological and physical aspects of life; and where there is warm affection and harmony among family members. A family which can strike a balance between these factors is indeed a happy family.

But when we look around us at the situation in most parts of the world, what do we see? Children loitering in the streets and video arcades. They play truant. Children are abused, wives are beaten and ageing parents are packed off to old folks homes regardless of their feelings. All these are tell-tale signs that all is not well at the most basic level of society: these are signs of social decadence.

It is a sad situation when good values and traditions are no longer practised. There is little interaction among members of the family and friends and the sense of responsibility towards other members of the family is weakening. Unhappiness in a family may be attributed to poverty, but having material wealth is no guarantee of happiness either, if it simply breeds selfishness, cruelty and greed.

A child learns affection and love from his parents and, together, they make a happy family unit. Through this microcosm of society, it learns about caring, sharing, compassion and concern for others. Throughout the ages religion has been an important force to organize these values into a system that is easily recognized and taught. Thus family and religion are vital components in imparting and nurturing these values.

The family plays an important role in the development of its members. The best of Asian and Western cultures teach and practise respect for elders, compassion for the sick and needy, care for elderly parents and consideration for the young.

Children growing up in families practising these values will emulate them and act accordingly towards others. But given the vast technological advances in modern civilization we are fast losing these values. Something must be done to bring the family back together and save society.

We must protect and support family development as an institution in the light of the rapid demographic and socio-economic changes world-wide. Extended families are giving way to nuclear families. We can do little to stop this trend but the values of respect, concern and compassion must be preserved. Good values, both Eastern and Western, must be maintained despite changes in lifestyle brought on by modernisation, industrialisation and urbanisation.

The mother is an important figure in family development. As care, love, tenderness and compassion are her innate qualities, she imparts these sterling values to her children in their upbringing. The mother, because of her love, concern, compassion, patience and tolerance thus holds the family together. Her espousal of these values may be passed on to her children who are great imitators and who learn by examples. We must as a group reinstate the traditional function of the mother, although of course to suit modern needs and pressures.

Religion too, promotes good human values. Strong resilient families and the practice of religion are therefore necessary in the promotion of family development.

It could be said that a happy family is a group of people living amicably and peacefully together with emphasis on religion, discipline and parenthood to create a happy family atmosphere. Values like these should be upheld and religiously protected so that a family is not influenced by anti-social values and unacceptable norms.

Realistic and reasonable parents make for a happy family. And the only way parents can build a happy family is through the institution of marriage. It worked very well in the past. It can do so now, provided we make it relevant to the needs of today's living.

Marital Problems

Almost every day, we hear of people complaining about their marriages. Young people reading romantic novels and seeing romantic films often conclude that marriage is a bed of roses. Unfortunately, marriage is not as sweet as one thinks. Marriage and marital problems are inter-related and people must remember that when they get married, they will have to face certain problems and responsibilities that they never expected or experienced before.

After the euphoria of the wedding, the realities of living together will set in for the couple, and for some, the prospects are daunting. Lack of communication or interaction with members of a family are some of the factors which can be attributed to an unhappy marriage. A stage will be reached when husband and wife do not even communicate with each other.

Common examples of non-communication between husband and wife are : (a) even at the breakfast table he is deeply engrossed in the newspaper; (b) when he returns from work he will be engrossed with his hobbies or watches television, and during weekends goes for golf or indulges in other pastimes; (c) he does not express any feelings or concern for the wife, let alone observing important anniversaries or birthdays.

The wife on her part, after getting married, is no longer interested in her figure and general appearance. She dresses shabbily. As she no longer reads or maintains a stimulating circle of friends, the husband finds that he can no longer engage in a stimulating conversation with her. Life then becomes boring and this leads the husband to resort to drink and seek solace outside the matrimonial home.

When does discontent first creep into a marriage? For most couples, the first year is usually a good year. For some couples, the adjustments of living together as husband and wife may turn out to be a stressful experience. The arrival of the first child could also give rise to problems as both man and wife grapple with the realities of being first-time parents.

Some people say that the first year after their marriage the husband would listen to his wife. From the second year the wife would listen to her husband. From the third year onwards neighbours would listen to both of them when they shout at each other.

Usually, discontent will be greater if there is no adequate preparation for marriage. For instance, pre-marital counselling will help couples prepare for the many surprises, pleasant or otherwise, that they may discover in the course of their marriage.

The dissatifaction that is supposed to hit most men after being married for so many years arises from a misconception that 'the grass is greener on the other side of the fence.' This tendency to be attracted to members of the opposite sex has no age limits. Such restlessness can occur anytime during the marriage, even for women.

Boredom is the usual cause, whereas disappointment with the partner is also a common complaint. When expectations are not fulfilled, pockets of grouses will start to develop. In any case, when there is no firm commitment to the marriage and no religious foundation, anything can happen at anytime to jeopardise it.

What are the roots of discontent? Many wives say that they wish their husbands would listen to them more, be more attentive to their needs or express their feelings better. It all boils down to a case of communication which is very much lacking in most modern marriages. In the past because of their up–bringing women were content to remain in the background and accept any kind of treatment at the hands of their husbands. But times have changed. Women are much better educated, hold responsible jobs are knowledgeable of their rights. Men must accept these realities and treat their wives as equal partners in a marriage. They can no longer be taken for granted.

For most men, marriage is a goal which they set for themselves to achieve. Having done so, they will pour their energies and time into the other most important aspect of their lives, that is, their career or business.

The expectations of the woman, on the other hand are totally different. After being married, she expects more love and intimacy and therefore seeks to spend more time with her husband.

Bringing one's outside problems to the home and taking it out on the spouse and children is damaging to the family's stability and creates a stress spiral.

In Asian societies, the problem of in-law interference is a common one. This is particularly so if the in-laws are able to influence the decisions of their child. A common complaint put forward by wives is that the husbands listen to their parents instead of to them. The interference of the in-laws in the upbringing of the children is also a common problem. While the grand-parents tend to be relaxed with the children and sometimes spoil them, the conflict of values between generations is often glaring in such cases.

Some young couples are not happy to

allow their children to have close association with their grand parents thinking they will learn the old fashioned way of life of their grand parents.

In India and Sri Lanka and to a lesser extent even in Malaysia, the dowry system is one of the main obstacles to a happy union. The dowry could include huge amounts of money, a bungalow, a luxury car, all of these or even more, depending on how affluent the parents are. And because parents want desperately to marry their daughters off, they make promises which they cannot keep and the marriage starts to crumble.

The dowry system has been abused. In the old days, a dowry was given to the daughter for safekeeping in case of an emergency. Then, unlike today, women were totally dependent on their husbands and the dowry was a kind of insurance in case the husband became unable to support her. Later, the dowry was to be handed over to the in-laws for safekeeping and now it has become compulsory for the daughter-in-law's parents to present her future in-laws with the dowry.

People often think that it is a duty to get married and that marriage is a very important part of their lives. However, in order to ensure a successful marriage, a couple has to harmonise their lives by minimising whatever differences they may have between them. A couple must also learn to accept each other's shortcomings and personal weaknesses. Even happy, well-matched couples can experience conflict, hurt, disappointment and anger. They may recognise shortcomings in such areas as showing appreciation of each other, willingness to converse and expressing emotions clearly. Do not shy away from conflict. Disagreements can lead to marital growth, not distance. Quarrels are essential for survival in a healthy marriage. But a quarrel can only be successfully terminated if both parties can forgive and forget.

Be willing to work at your marriage. Do not assume that since the first 10 or 20 years were good, the next 10 or 20 will also be good. Love needs to be fed — with shared experiences, joys and sorrows. This requires time, attention, courage and understanding.

One of the major causes of marital problems is suspicion and mistrust. Both husband and wife should show implicit trust for one another and try not to have secrets between them. Secrets create suspicion, suspicion leads to jealousy, jealousy generates anger, anger causes enmity and enmity may result in separation or divorce, suicide or even murder.

If a couple can share pain and pleasure in their day-to-day life, they can console each other and minimise their grievances. Thus, the wife or husband should not expect to experience only pleasure in their wedded lives. There will be a lot of painful, miserable episodes, burdens and misunderstandings. Discussing mutual problems with one another will give them confidence to resolve any obstacle that they will have to face. They must have the strong will-power to reduce tension and develop the confidence to live together with better understanding and tolerance.

Men and women need the comfort of each other when facing problems and difficulties. The feeling of insecurity and unrest will disappear and life will be more meaningful, happy and interesting if there is someone who is willing to share the other's burden.

Marital problems prompted a cynic to say that there can only be a peaceful married life if the marriage is between a blind wife and a deaf husband, for the blind wife cannot see the faults of the husband and a deaf husband cannot hear the nagging of his wife.

Living Together Outside Marriage

Living together before getting married, or cohabiting as it is more commonly known, is a cosy option among young people in the West, and is progressively catching on in many Asian countries. It is said that about half of the couples in the United States and Britain would have lived together before marriage. One can learn about it in the movies and in the papers. In the conservative East, on the other hand, living together before marriage is still very much a taboo. The mere mention of the subject is enough to be frowned upon particularly by the elders. We must add however that as the world is shrinking so fast many of these values are being adopted in the East as well, especially in urban areas.

In the United States, where living together out of wedlock is becoming increasingly acceptable, one out of three marriages results in divorce.

Tragic cases do occur in situations where couples live together out of wedlock, for example when the female partner gets pregnant and the male partner later disclaims responsibility. This often leads to the problem of unwed mothers.

Problem of Unwed Mothers

Media reports of unwed mothers abandoning or discarding their babies at rubbish dumps, bushes or into toilets, drains and streams are just too dreadful for any caring, right-thinking member of society to condone. With such reports appearing almost every other day, the public is alarmed, saddened and have called for remedial measures to check the growing problem which has reached alarming proportions.

Some abandoned babies survive only because they are found in time by garbage collectors, residents or passers-by, although they had been exposed to such dangers as stray dogs, rats, ants and the elements of cold/heat. One wonders how these mothers can abandon their babies, as even animals are known to be fiercely protective of their offspring. It has to be remembered that not all babies born out of wedlock are from young girls. Adult women too are guilty of this terrible practice.

Parents should try to understand their children. They should ensure that their children will turn to them whenever they have a problem.

People who abandon their babies need help. They need counselling. We should not simply blame the West every time some problems crop up here. No doubt our youngsters are getting more and more westernised in their thinking, outlook, lifestyle and actions. Here is where the role of parents comes in.

Some parents are too busy working that they unintentionally neglect their children. Hence, parents should spend more time to instil discipline and educate their children on what is wrong and right.

We need a humane approach in dealing with the problem of unwed mothers which could start with the family where parents and children do not communicate well. When it happens to a daughter, she is afraid of being penalised, of not being accepted by the family and society as well as the social stigma attached to her; and she has nobody to turn to for advice or help. She is already paying for her mistake by shouldering the burden alone. Her parents also do not accept her and society condemns her and as a result she becomes desperate.

To overcome this problem, family development efforts must be stepped up where couples will be trained to be better parents, and young people will be responsible for themselves through programmes on sex education. Religious bodies and religious counsellors can greatly assist the government to fight this terrible social disease.

Sexual Exploitation of Children and Child Labour

Child prostitution is one of the fastest growing businesses in many countries. Tour agencies and affluent travellers have brought about this state of affairs to a large extent.

'Sex has become a multi-billion-dollar

industry and today children are being bought, sold and traded like any other mass product,' deplores Aaron Sachs, a staff researcher at the Washington – based World Institute.

'At 10, you are a woman. At 20, you are an old woman. And at 30, you are dead.' Thus goes a popular saying in certain countries.

In the ever expanding sex market, child prostitutes are among the hottest commodities. This is particularly true in Asia, the centre of the child sex industry. The Progress of Nations 1995 report of the United Nations Children's Fund (UNICEF) lists Thailand as the third country with the most number of child prostitutes. About 100,000 children are selling sex in this country. The record holder is India with 400,000 to 500,000 children. The United States is second with 300,000. The Philippines is fourth with 60,000.

'The number of under 18s involved in prostitution probably exceeds two million,' the report says. 'Best estimates suggest a figure of one million for Asia alone, and 300,000 for the United States.'

Although most of the child prostitutes are girls, in many parts of the world even boys are used for sex.

Rich tourists, according to an official of the non-government watch group ECPAT (End Child Prostitution in Asian Tourism), 'have realised that human life is cheaper in the Third World.'

Why has child prostitution become popular in recent years? One possible reason is the fear of being infected by HIV, the virus that causes the dreaded Acquired Immuno-deficiency Syndrome (AIDS).

Sex tourists think children are AIDS-free. 'With the growing fear of HIV infection, many people are always on the search for younger and younger victims, and the demand unfortunately has been met by the 'ever-eager middleman,' observes Ramesh Shrestha, a UNICEF official based in Hanoi, Vietnam.

Experts cite poverty as the reason children are forced into the sex trade. 'Children are attracted to prostitution because it pays better than odd jobs,' Philippine Senator Ernesto F. Herrera said in his recent privilege speech. Children of the streets of Rio, Nairobi, Manila and Bombay often get involved in prostitution in order to survive and not by choice, a world congress against sexual exploitation of children observed. The congress has cast a harsh light on the conditions of poor children around the world, being forced out in life to find work without any schooling.

In some other countries, street children are among the first to be recruited into prostitution and often kept in brothels. Others drift into prostitution on a more casual basis and not as part of any network. With no family they simply have to find a way to survive. Social dislocation push these children into a means of earning a living, which they know is dishonourable but provides a more comfortable compensation.

In Latin America, street children come from among the poorest families, often from violent areas, frequently thrown out by the family, according to Per-Erik Astrom of the Swedish branch of the 'Save the Children Fund'. He said: 'A child of 15 in Rio, if he has lived that long, knows everything about survival, owns two younger sisters and has become a pimp himself!'

A Chilean organisation, CERSO report: 'Mothers send their children on to the streets to beg although they know the dangers that the girls may end up as drug addicts and prostitutes.' For more than 10 years now, Ladawan Wongsriwong, a two-time Member of Parliament from the northern Thailand province of Payao, has been fighting against child prostitution, an industry estimated to be worth US$1.5 billion (RM3.6 billion) annually.

Her crusade against this social ill involves a four-pronged strategy that includes a campaign to make people understand the causes, effects and ways to check the problem.

'Although people generally have more understanding of the problem, there are parents who still hang on to the old idea that prostitution is indeed a good career fetching a high income for their daughters. We are trying to change all that by also having training workshops, meetings and seminars with parents as well as dissemination of information through the mass media', says Ladawan, 40, who is from Thailand's opposition Democrat Party and President of the Young Northern Women's Development Foundation.

Ladawan says for the legislation to work effectively, it is imperative that all countries come to an agreement and co-operate to consider women and child abuse as a criminal offence because the child prostitution problem is not only the making of Thai people alone, as foreigners have a part in it too.

The demand from European tourists and those from other developed countries for young girls seems limitless. According to the international children's advocacy group, Terre Des Hommes, each year tens of thousands of sex tourists from Germany alone visit Thailand, with about 10% of them engaging in sex with minors. It is a fact that young girls from poor families, who are deprived of continuing their education at secondary level, are being lured into prostitution.

It has been reported that a Swiss business man sexually abused 1500 children in Sri Lanka within a period of eight years!

There is a growing industry of commercial sexual exploitation of children for pornographic purposes. Thailand has the highest record of child trafficking and juvenile pornography. This accounts for the most profane type of paedophile material available in illicit video collections containing scenes of homosexual paedophilic depravity.

The recent discovery of a gruesome kidnapping and paedophilic ring in Belgium has awakened public opinion and dramatically illustrated the fact that sexual exploitation of children is not a problem only in Thailand, Brazil, Bangladesh, India and Sri Lanka; it exists practically in every country including Europe. The World Congress against commercial sexual exploitation of children has initiated co-operation at local, national and international levels to combat the child sex problem. Considering the level of international commitments, the World Congress has outlined priorities for the prevention, protection, rehabilitation and reintegration of child victims of sexual exploitation.

The term 'child labour' is defined as the employment of boys and girls when they are too young to work for hire, or when they are employed at jobs unsuitable or unsafe for children of their ages or under conditions injurious to their welfare. The term has had different meanings at various times and in various communities, depending on society's concept of its responsibility for its youth.

In Malaysia, the employment of children is governed by the provisions of the Children and Young Persons (Employment) Act 1966, which state that a child, or any person below 14 years of age, may not be employed except under certain strict conditions, such as light work suitable for his or her capacity in any undertaking carried out by the family. Under separate conditions, such as employment in shops the child must not be less than 16 years old.

The Malaysian Labour Department has intensified its enforcement activities in the light of increasing complaints involving illegal child labour, especially during the school holidays. The illegal employment of children stems primarily from the acute shortage of labour in the country. The enforcement activities of the department have been intensified nation-wide through scheduled inspections, as well as surprise raids both during the day and night.

Child experts at a regional meeting

in Manila said they needed not just more resources for children's welfare, but also greater involvement of the media in conveying the plight of Asia's vulnerable children to policymakers.

'Children who are poor, exploited or forced to work, remind the world that economic growth has not given them the benefits of prosperity,' said Pratima Kale, Regional Director of the United Nations Children's Fund (UNICEF) for East Asia and the Pacific. 'The situations of inequity can and often do lead to anger, frustration and violence if their basic needs are not met; if their basic rights are not fulfilled; and if they do not see any hope for the future,' she said at the start of the Asian Summit on Child Rights and Media.

SEX DEVIATIONS

Sex deviations, sometimes called sexual aberrations, have concerned mankind almost from earliest recorded history. It is customary to refer to persons exhibiting what we could call sexual deviations, or departures from what modern society agrees to be normal, as sex perverts. Thus many persons, otherwise well informed in their own minds, have categorised and speak of them casually as perverts, sexual psychopaths, sex neurotics and so on, often without understanding very clearly the condition to which they refer. Our social customs seem to compel society to look upon a sex deviant as one bringing disgrace to his family.

Sex deviations such as homosexuality, bisexuality, transvestism have long been taboo subjects rarely brought up in polite conversation by respectable society. Strange as it may seem, teenagers today however are far more well-informed and open minded in their views on this subject.

More often than not, one associates the word 'homosexual' with effeminate men or men in drag. This is the stereotypical image of homosexuality that, like most stereotypes, conveniently obscures its complexity.

The word 'homosexuality' applies to people who are sexually and emotionally attracted to others of the same sex. Both men and women can be called 'homosexual' or 'gay', but these are only umbrella terms under which lie many shades of distinctions. Broadly speaking, homosexuals comprise gay men, transvestites (both male and female), trans-sexuals (female and male) and lesbians.

And to complicate things further, there is a very fine distinction between the interchangable terms, 'transvestite' and 'trans-sexual'. As most dictionaries explain it, a transvestite is a person who dresses in the clothes of the opposite sex, often deriving gratification from this practice.

On the other hand, a trans-sexual is (as commonly understood) someone who has decided to live as a person of the opposite sex. Sometimes, a trans-sexual's identification with the opposite sex is so strong that he or she goes for a sex-change operation.

Some people who practise transvestism may not be gay; they may just enjoy wearing the clothes of the opposite sex without being sexually attracted to members of the same sex.

A gay is attracted to men of his own kind – gays, and not 'straight' men. When asked why a normal looking man would fall in love with another, he would say that there is nothing abnormal about him. Most people however find it difficult to accept gays as normal people.

Transvestites and trans-sexuals, on the other hand, consider themselves, and are considered by the gay community, as women. They generally feel that they are women trapped in male bodies. And as women, they are attracted to straight men, and not to gay men.

The world is indeed very much a lonely and hostile place for transvestites and trans-sexuals. It is difficult for them to have meaningful relationships as very few straight men are willing to face the social stigma and emotional hassles that come with having a transvestite partner.

What causes a person to be gay? According to some researchers, sexual and emotional attraction for a partner of the same sex may be a genetic trait, although social factors and upbringing are also thought to play a role. Homosexuality is not a medical or psychiatric disorder, although regarded as abnormal by many. Homosexuality was removed from the list of mental disorders in the early 1970s when it was obvious that homosexuals are as psychologically well-adjusted as heterosexuals are. They have the same capacity to function in society, to achieve goals, to have their needs met, and to develop a sense of identity.

However, transvestism is considered a mental disorder, as transvestites have the feeling of being trapped in a man's body, causing a lot of inner turmoil, whereas gay men are totally comfortable with their maleness.

Although homosexuals may have accepted their sexual orientation, society may not be ready to accept them. They may be prepared to share their thoughts and feelings with family members and close friends, but not so in public. A homosexual person may go through several stages before coming to terms with himself or herself. They probably can't do anything about their 'condition', and we should not contribute to the prevailing social pressure that forces many of them to hide their true selves in the closet. From the Buddhist point of view this kind of sexual act can be regarded as sexual misconduct to those who try to renounce sensual pleasure in order to lead a holy life. For others this can be regarded as sex abuse.

BREAST FEEDING
OF THE CHILD AND ITS ADVANTAGES

The modern attitude of working mothers towards their children tend to erode the time honoured filial piety which children are expected to maintain. The replacement of breast feeding by bottle feeding is yet another cause. When mothers breast feed and cuddle babies in their arms, the tender affection between mother and child becomes much greater. A breast feeding mother, through her maternal instinct, often experiences a tremendous satisfaction from knowing she is providing her baby, as nature had intended, with something of her very own which no one else can give. The influence a mother has on the child thus grows and becomes much more pronounced. Under such circumstances, filial piety, family cohesion and obedience are invariably enhanced.

A variety of arguments have been advanced to convince mothers that 'breast is best'. The reasons include both physiological and psychological advantages for the infant and the mother as well. The protein and other ingredients in human milk differ qualitatively from the protein in cow's milk. Breast milk is sterile and is not subject to contamination. Breast fed infants are more resistant to infections and communicable diseases. They are also less susceptible to allergic reactions. It is also cheaper to breast feed an infant than to purchase formula milk for bottle feeding. Breast feeding offers a superior psychological intimacy that results in emotional and cognitive advantages over other feeding methods. Breast-feeding also facilitates the development of mother-infant relationships and bonding.

Breast feeding the new born is more practical and less time-consuming than bottle feeding. There is no need for bottle sterilisers and washing. The milk supply is ready whenever the baby needs it. Babies who are breastfed have been found to cry less in the later months of the first year compared with those who are bottle-fed. Remember, nothing is more rewarding than the love between parent and child. Making time for your baby is definitely worth it.

During the early days following birth, breastfeeding provides the baby with the benefits of colostrum. Colostrum is the Pre-milk substance secreted by the breasts until milk is produced, usually about the second or third postpartum day. Colostrum is rich in all of the baby's essential needs.

Breast milk provides all the nutrition and vitamins the baby needs for at least the first six months after birth. Breast milk contains immunology factors that help prevent a host of diseases and allergies. Except in extreme circumstances, as in the case of mothers who suffer from AIDS and who can transmit the sickness to their babies, there is no real substitute for mothers' milk.

Also, physical contact with the mother evidently adds to the satisfaction of feeding. Authorities in various fields of child development have insisted that the breast is the only satisfactory way of feeding an infant. Breast feeding is recommended as many physicians believe it offers an advantage to the baby, physiologically as well as emotionally, because of the definite advantages that result from the mother's own satisfaction in nursing her baby. The baby needs affectionate handling, plenty of time and a relaxed atmosphere, just as much as the milk itself.

These traditional traits are for the good and well-being of children. It is up to the parents, especially the mother to provide them with love, care and affection as their rightful dues. The mother is responsible for the child being good or wayward. The mother can thus reduce juvenile delinquency!

'Those who lead their lives by going against nature, must face the consequences either physically or mentally'.

Birth Control

Planned parenthood or voluntary parenthood under the Family Planning Programme refers to the regulation of conception within the family and is often referred to as birth control. Planned parenthood refers to the regulation and spacing of offspring by legal and ethical means, depending on the health, economic condition and circumstances of husband and wife.

One must take into consideration the fact that a controlled birth rate is conducive to sane living. Rapidly increasing population is a dangerous trend that creates problems in the wake of people marching towards sufficiency and secure living.

In Asia, where generations of people

continue to live in sub-human conditions, it is appropriate to take advantages of Family Planning, in so far as it does not come into conflict with communal problems. A country that is able to support itself enjoys the greatest freedom.

There is no reason for Buddhists to oppose birth control. They are at liberty to use any of the old or modern methods to prevent conception. Those who object to birth control by saying that it is against God's law to practise it, must realise that their concept regarding this issue is not very reasonable. In birth control what is done is to prevent the coming into being of an existence, and hence there is no killing involved.

Abortion

Although a person has the freedom to plan a family according to his own conviction, abortion is however not justifiable. This action is wrong because it involves the taking away or destroying of a visible or invisible life.

The word abortion evokes images of desperate young women and back-street abortionists. To many, the word also carries an illegal and criminal connotation. In the developed West the issue has been politicised as well.

Abortion is defined as the expulsion of a foetus from the uterus, brought about by accidental means or induction, before it is capable of carrying on its own life. In medical terms, abortion is the termination of pregnancy up to the 28th week of gestation. After this period, the foetus is regarded medically as viable, and any subsequent expulsion of the unborn human being may either be a live birth or a still birth.

In law, when abortion is committed with malicious intent, it becomes a criminal offence and the party causing it may be charged and punished. When an abortion results in the death of the woman, the crime is designated as murder.

The abortion issue has always remained contentious, but for women faced with an unwanted pregnancy, the matter is neither illegal nor political. It is personal and one which has to be dealt with quickly, at whatever cost. Under certain circumstances, such women in desperate situations may feel compelled to resort to abortion. But they should not justify this act of abortion, for somehow or other they will have to face the adverse consequences of committing such a cruel act.

In this country, ending a pregnancy is permitted only when it has been ascertained that the mother's physical or mental health is in danger. The procedure is referred to as therapeutic abortion and it requires the certification of two medical practitioners. Any other request for induced abortions would contravene the law.

Religious principles should never be surrendered for the satisfaction of humankind. Rather they should stand for the welfare of mankind as a whole.

Domestic Violence

The problem of domestic violence affecting families, particularly in the lower income group, and in certain, cases even in affluent societies, has reached alarming proportions. It has become necessary for the Government to legislate action, resulting in the recent passing of the Domestic Violence Act by Parliament in June 1996.

Evidence shows that a battered wife in many cases still loves her husband despite all the abuses, which she puts down to his alcoholism, gambling, womanising and constant financial problems. This is the reality of the problem of domestic violence faced by a large number of women today. Many a battered wife just endures it because she firmly believes that any retaliation on her part might end in her losing custody of her children, and her right to inherit the matrimonial home and to enjoy any form of financial security.

The public generally holds the view that domestic violence is a matter that does not warrant any outside intervention. For instance, neighbours will quickly come to a woman's aid if they hear her scream that she is being burgled, but when she screams from her husband's constant battery, others are reluctant to intervene as they consider it a personal family matter. Until very recently this view was also held by the police. Under the Domestic Violence Act however, police duties now include escorting the abused spouse home to collect her belongings, if necessary. What abused wives ask for is protection under the law, and not so much that their husbands be punished.

The Act gives protection to the abused spouse without breaking up the family. Under the Act one would be able to get a court order barring the abusive spouse from the matrimonial home, providing maintenance to the abused spouse and children as well as giving her custody of the children. The Act makes domestic violence a punishable offence.

Divorce – Only as a Last Resort
Divorce is a controversial issue among the followers of different religions. Some people believe that marriage is recorded in heaven

and therefore human beings have no right to allow divorce. But, if a husband and wife really cannot live together, instead of leading a miserable life and generating more conflict, anger and hatred, they should have the liberty to separate and live apart peacefully.

Separation or divorce is not prohibited in Buddhism though the necessity would scarcely arise if the Buddha's injunctions were strictly followed. Men and women must have the liberty to separate if they really cannot agree with each other. Separation is preferred to suffering a miserable family life for a long period of time.

Some may prefer legal separation which is a kind of divorce except that the marriage exists in name for various reasons.

Factors contributing to divorce vary. When the flame of love suddenly dies or when the vow to 'love, honour and cherish each other for life' seems no longer possible to maintain, divorce appears to be the best solution. Of course, there are other factors too, ranging from extra-marital affairs, in-law problems as well as family differences faced by working mothers related to the pursuit of a career. In this connection, we are reminded of the Buddha's advice that old men should not marry young wives as it can create incompatibility, jealousy and suspicion

(Parabhava Sutta).

Under the Law Reform (Marriage and Divorce) Act 1976, and with effect from 1 March 1982, Marriage Tribunals have also been set up throughout Malaysia with functions to resolve and to reconcile couples, other than those of the Muslim faith, who have marital difficulties. (Couples of the Muslim faith are separately governed by Syariah Law and come under the jurisdiction of the Syariah Court).

Marriage Tribunals have been set up in every State, including the Federal Territory of Kuala Lumpur. The Act makes it mandatory to refer a matrimonial difficulty to the Marriage Tribunal set up under the Act before a divorce petition can be filed.

The Act provides a time frame of six months to see if the couple can reach a settlement. Every Tribunal has to meet the statutory requirement of three or four hearings per case within the six-monthly period. If there are no signs of reconciliation, the Tribunal will issue a certificate to that effect to the petitioner. It is only after the certificate is issued that a petitioner can file a divorce petition in the High Court through a lawyer.

Unfortunately, when parents get divorced, their children become the innocent victims who suffer the worst consequences of that failed marriage. Divorce is a social phenomenon and is something which affects the children psychologically and could make them feel insecure. They have to cope with innumerable problems of acceptance, adjustment and insecurity. Such young children will need constant counselling and constant moral support and comfort to ride out this very traumatic phase in their lives.

Divorced parents are often portrayed as selfish hedonists interested only in their own happiness, and not their children's.

Some may have to live with a stepparent when their parents remarry and will have to make new living arrangements. Divorce is almost like denying child the right to have a fulfilled life with both biological parents under one roof. Because of their disturbed minds, these children could lose concentration and as a result their performance in school could be affected. This will runaway children and juvenile crime.

Very often when the divorce had been unpleasant and having suffered physically at the hands of their angry parents, children grow up being afraid of entering into marriage themselves in later life because they view it as threatening their safety and holding little hope for happiness. They have lost trust in their parents for breaking up the marriage and they also lack trust in the opposite sex.

For some children, the emotional scars may heal with time. But for others, they may remain. Divorce therefore affects not just two people but many other innocent parties as well. There must be powerful reasons before anyone seeks to resort to divorce.

Most children of divorced parents would occasionally cherish and harbour the secret wish that they would get reconciled and family life becomes normal again.

Utmost care must be taken to ensure that separation is done in an atmosphere of goodwill and understanding by adopting reasonable solutions and not by creating more hatred. In fact they should make every effort to part amicably as friends. If a couple has children, they should try to make the divorce less traumatic for them and help them to adjust to the new situation. It is most important to ensure that their future and welfare will be well taken care of. It is inhuman if the couple desert their children and allow them to fend for themselves and lead a miserable life.

When a man for whatever reason institutes divorce proceedings it is the woman who more often than not will be the most hurt in the process. Her cherished dream of a happy married life would be shattered, particularly so if the husband, involved in an extra-marital affair, is seeking release from the marriage vows to be with the 'other woman.' A woman facing impending divorce would often express her frustrated feelings which is typical in such tragic cases: 'I was devastated. For me the world had come to an end and I thought about dying to make him regret for not wanting me'.

The dilemma faced by many divorced women in Malaysia is the sad fact that she has only the right to care for her child but has no authority as legal guardian. In connection with this predicament, mothers who have custody of their children are forced to appeal to their ex-husbands to exercise what should be their (the mothers') right in the first place. What if the father does not co-operate by giving his consent or if he cannot be traced? The unfortunate child, who may need a passport to study abroad for example will be left in a quandary.

The only way a mother will ever get to be the legal guardian of her child is when the father dies, is declared insane or has a criminal record. Under the circumstances, lawyers generally advise women to start applying for custody and guardianship as soon as they are separated from their husbands, and not wait until divorce proceedings start, but this is never an easy process.

DISCRIMINATION AGAINST WOMEN

The Buddha says that if we are to understand anything, we must learn to 'see things as they are'. It is after such analysis of women in relation to men, that He came to the conclusion that there is no impediment in women to enable them to practise religion as men do and attain the highest state in life, which is Arahanthood or Sainthood, the highest level of mental purity. The Buddha had to face strong opposition in giving full freedom to women to practise religion.

At the time of the Buddha, before He emancipated women, the customs and traditions were such that the women were considered as chattel, to be used by men at their pleasure. Manu, the ancient law-giver of India, had decreed that women were inferior to men. Women's position in society was therefore very low, and it was restricted to the kitchen. They were not even allowed to enter temples and to participate in religious activities in any manner whatsoever.

As we have previously noted under the heading 'Birth Control', discrimination against females begins even before the child is born into this world! The widespread practice of female foeticide prevalent in many parts of the world today testifies to this horrifying fact. Further on, under the heading 'Women's Liberation Movement and its Effect on Family Life', the discrimination against women in affluent societies, particularly those aspiring for top managerial positions in the corporate sector, will be dealt with in detail.

In developing and underdeveloped countries however, the situation can only be described as being far worse and more deplorable as the following accounts will reveal.

In India's ritualistic, male dominated society, widowhood is a terrible fate for a woman. There are numerous cases of widows (some still in their 20s) who were cast away from their families and shunned by society after their husbands died.

Among superstitious families, a widow often is blamed by her in-laws for her husband's death and is even ostracised. There are few options left for widows. Hindus frown on remarriage for women, although there are no such barriers for men. Until modern times, widows were expected to jump on to the funeral pyre of their husbands according to a tradition known as *sati*. Although the practice was outlawed by the British several decades ago, the last known case occurred as recently as 1996. Most women in India have little to look forward to when they become widows.

One typical tragic example could be cited of a widow who underwent child marriage which is another custom prevalent in rural India. She laments: 'I was married off when I was only five years old. My husband, whom I never saw, was 13 and he died one month after the wedding. I am now a widow.'

According to the World Bank, 65% of Indian women older than 60 are widows. That figure rises to 80% for women older than 70.

The All India Democratic Women's Association reports that in India where a woman's identity is determined by her being an appendage to a male, widowhood has much larger implications than just losing a husband.

The situation is no better even in some other neighbouring countries. For a long time, families regarded daughters as inferior to sons and treated them accordingly. A girl is generally seen as suitable only for household chores. She lives through a series of social practices which generate, breed and reinforce discrimination against her. She becomes an economic burden and a moral liability. Yet, she is expected to raise healthy, hardworking and educated children and be a good mother. Many little boys grow up thinking their sisters are inferior having seen them treated less well than themselves. These beliefs are reinforced by many members of the society, including women themselves.

Perhaps the single biggest issue is the lack of support and the restrictions girls face if they want to do something with their lives beyond the traditional roles assigned to them as domestic help, baby-sitters for younger siblings, cooks and cleaners. In effect, girls are under life-long training to be good wives when they grow up.

As a 16 year old girl from Rawalpindi, points out: 'Our society does not treat girls well. People here do not educate their girls because to them girls are not theirs. Girls are seen as belonging to their future in-laws' families and any investment in their future is futile. They go to their husbands' homes at a young age, usually anywhere from 13. The rest of their lives is spent looking after in-laws, and bearing and bringing up children to prolong and strengthen their husband's family line.'

We need to eradicate this type of thinking and make education compulsory and free so that it does not become an issue' she says. 'Girls should also be able to have jobs, working in places where no one disapproves and preferably with other girls so parents can't object. I have always regretted that I was born a girl. Sometimes when I was not allowed to do something I would go to my room, cry and pray to God to make me a boy.'

The Girl Child Project in such countries is slowly changing all this by developing a core of young girls to act as catalysts in creating local awareness of the problems of girls and the discrimination they face.

The issue of education crops up almost invariably. Many girls have had to fight for their right to education. Some were helped in this fight by their untutored mothers who believed that their own lives would have been better if they had had some schooling.

In many societies a woman's place is in the home; a married woman owes her first allegiance to her duties as wife and mother. There is no such thing as 'women's lib'. Even in some progressive societies women are humiliated. For example in public places, they are required not only to sit apart from the men, but out of their view — that is, behind them. When women are placed at the back of a room or hall, it acts as a subtle indication that their expected role is 'behind' and not 'together with' that of the men.

Some people believe that women are prone to evil. Therefore, it would be better to get them do more domestic work so that they can forget their natural evil attitude.

Women's Liberation Movement and its Effect on Family Life

In the distant past men went out to hunt for food for the family and the women remained at home to cook and take care of the children and the home. Hence the origin of the popular phrase: 'A woman's place is in the home.'

In the old days, women were quite content being home makers. They did not go out to work or pursue a career. The stereotype of womanhood — a life that revolves around children and kitchen — has eroded over the past several decades, as more and more women have pursued careers. Rural society in general however still promotes motherhood and not careerism. Society accepts quite generally the fact that the single woman worker ordinarily supports herself and she contributes largely to the support of aged parents and younger members of the family. Most women seek employment because of economic needs and changing attitudes about personal fulfilment.

However with the call for women's liberation, many women seem to think that the solution is to compete with men outside the home. Such women should consider very carefully whether they want to bear children, or to pursue a career. It is irresponsible for a mother to bring a life into this world and then leave it in the care of others without due consideration for its welfare. You are responsible for what you create.

There has been a notable increase of married women who are employed. Today, they have forged ahead as career women, often playing a dual role of working woman and mother. Most working mothers are torn between the guilt of leaving their children at home with servants and the call of their careers.

With more and more women doing further studies, the number of working mothers is increasing. Over the years, women have made substantial advances in the professions and now occupy important top management positions in government departments and in 'the private sector. The trend is most pronounced in the urban areas. In the political field women have risen to top ministerial positions, to the extent that they find themselves more in the limelight of public life, whilst their husbands in the background, have to be content and remained in the shadows of their wives.

Women executives climbing the corporate ladder to top management positions however still face subtle form of sex discrimination. The gender gap faced by aspiring women, particularly professionals, is most pronounced at the top of the corporate ladder. Boardroom decisions usually end up with the remark: 'We are reluctant to groom them for leadership jobs because our investment is lost if they leave to become mothers.'

Gender discrimination at the executive level however is not easy to prove; hence the term 'glass ceiling' has been coined to describe the invisible but rigid barrier that blocks women's path to the upper echelons of corporate power. Although some people categorically deny the existence of such a barrier, women's routes to the top are blocked by this so called 'glass ceiling'. Hence to reach the top a woman has to make a choice between career and family. Some conscientious working mothers, with domestic helpers to look after the babies, have come to realise they could never leave their babies at the mercy of strange women; so however much they enjoy their office work they decide to give up their careers. It is indeed sad that some women on the other hand have chosen to pursue their careers at the expense of their families.

A child has a right to be satisfied materially, but more importantly spiritually and psychologically. The provision of material comfort is secondary when compared to the provision of parental love and attention.

We know of many people from poor homes who in spite of their meagre income have brought up children well with plenty of love.

Conversely, many rich people have provided every material comfort for their children, but being deprived of parental love, these children have grown up to become psychologically and morally handicapped.

Some women may feel that advising them to concentrate on the upbringing of the family is below their dignity or something degrading and reflects the thinking of the old and the conservative. It is true that in the past, women have been treated very badly, but this was due more to ignorance on the part of men rather than to an inherent weakness in women. The Sanskrit word for a housewife is Gruhini which literally means 'leader of the house.' Certainly it does not imply that a woman is inferior. Rather it means a division of responsibility for the male and the female.

Women have been struggling for ages to gain equality with men in the field of education, the professions, politics and other avenues. They are now at par with men to a great extent. The male generally tends to be aggressive by nature and the female more emotional. In the domestic scene, particularly in the East, the male is more dominant as head of the family whilst the female tends to remain as a passive partner. Please remember, 'passive' here does not mean 'weak'. Rather it is a positive quality of 'modesty' and 'gentleness'. If man and woman maintain their masculine and feminine qualities inherited from nature and recognise their respective strengths and status, then such an attitude can contribute towards a congenial and mutual understanding between the sexes.

In this connection, Gandhi's remarks are very relevant: 'I believe in the proper education of woman. But I do believe that woman will not make her contribution to the world by mimicking or running a race with man. She can run the race, but she will not rise to the great heights she is capable of by mimicking man'. Here we can look at the wisdom of the ancient Chinese when they created the YIN and YANG symbol. The curved line which divides the dark and light segments show that opposites need not take confrontational stances. When one dominates the other recedes. When one side recedes the other dominates, and so both remain equal. Womem has to be the complement of man.

In certain countries, many husbands hand over their pay packets to their wives who handle domestic affairs. This leaves the man free to concentrate on what he can do best for the family. Since each partner knows clearly what his or her responsibilities are, there is no conflict between them. The atmosphere at home is thus happy and peaceful where their children can grow up well.

Of course, the husband must see to it that his partner is well cared for, that she is consulted on every family decision, that there is enough freedom for her to develop her own personality and that she has her own free time to pursue her personal interests. In this sense, husband and wife are both equally responsible for the welfare of their family. They should not be in competition with each other.

A mother should consider carefully whether she should continue as a working mother with all the attendant pitfalls or to be a housewife giving all her undivided attention, due affection and care to her growing children. Strangely, some modern mothers, particularly in certain countries with military regimes facing a shortage of manpower, are being trained to handle guns or other deadly weapons when they should be cuddling their children and training them to be good or law-abiding citizens.

In certain countries female soldiers often carry arms, though usually for self defence, and they are no longer restricted to the rear echelon. In the air, women now fly combat aircraft and attack helicopters, not just being drivers of military transports, but at home they still display their gentleness and caring natures especially with to children.

CHILDREN AND SEX EDUCATION

Teaching children the facts of sex and sexual development needs to be done with care, sensitivity and in a holistic manner. Coping with changes in sexual development is an issue every child must face, and the challenge is even more critical for children during their early formative years. Educators and parents must therefore regard sexuality as part of human drives and needs that must be correctly channelled.

The necessity for giving correct information about sexual development to children is of paramount importance. Children nowadays are exposed to knowledge about sex – through the mass media (often with gory details), books, through the Internet and also from their peers, and if they are not taught to differentiate between what is appropriate and what is not, they might end up exhibiting inappropriate behaviour. No parents will ever want their children to obtain information on sexual development from the gutter.

Parents can impart knowledge of sex to their children but such information needs to be tailored to the child's level of understanding — in this case, the mental age, which may not correspond to the child's chronological age. Children are very innocent and can easily be victims of sexual abuse in the hands of unscrupulous adults. The child may not even realize that he is being used as an object to gratify the deviant sexual needs of adults.

One important area is the need to inform children as to what constitutes 'appropriate and inappropriate touching'. The importance of giving such awareness to children is stressed on parents. The child needs to know who is allowed to touch him or her and when, and where; what a doctor can touch, situations the child should avoid, and how best to stop inappropriate conduct in the classroom.

Parents themselves need to be aware that inappropriate touching could also happen between relatives. For instance, parents usually tell their children to 'beware of strangers', yet studies have shown that in child sexual abuse cases, the majority of abusers are in fact known to the child, or are members of the child's own family.

As with other children in society, children

require open lines of communication with their parents. This would include openness in discussing issues connected with sex. If any untoward physical contact has occurred they should be comfortable in telling their parents about it, instead of being too ashamed or too afraid to reveal details.

Sex education is important because one cannot expect teenagers to follow rules blindly without knowing why they must follow them. One of the subjects they should be educated about is why they should abstain from sex until after marriage.Many people oppose sex education for children because they think that 'once you tell them about it, they will go out and abuse it.' It is significant to note that in Switzerland, sex education is taught in kinder-gartens and that country has the lowest number of teenage pregnancies in the world. What is vitally important is that children be taught responsible sexual behaviour from the time they are ready for such instruction. A sound sexual education will save the child untold stress from guilt, fear, remorse and retri-bution in the future.

CRIME NURSERY

'The most fertile grounds for nurturing crimes are families. In spite of all the measures taken to decrease crime rates, violent crimes are increasing in many families in modern, technologically advanced societies. Most of them learn to become criminals from the way they are being brought up.

In some countries, while adult crime rates have fallen somewhat, crimes committed by youths continue to rise. We learn from the mass media that many children take guns to their schools. Sometimes we hear that very young children even below the age of five, have shot their siblings or parents. Usually crimes among youths are related to drugs and alcohol, which are easily available to them in some homes. Criminals are not born, but made by misguided and inconsiderate families and by the environment in which they live.

It has become a 20th century fashion among many people to live together without getting married. In some cases, children born into such circumstances suffer from neglect. Quite often these children end up under the care and guidance of one parent, usually the mother. The parent who is more irresponsible leaves the children under the care of the other partner. Women, since they often experience discrimination, have to work twice as hard as their male counterparts to provide for themselves and their children. The modern global economy is such that women are more disadvantaged than even underprivileged men. As the entire social structure has taken a completely different route from that of the traditional one, support for the family is also almost non-existent in many countries. Women often suffer more as a result and their difficulties are reflected in families they try to raise.

Children brought up by single parents often don't receive enough parental love and care. Psychologically-troubled parents cannot give very sound emotional fulfillment to their children. These children's baby-sitters sometimes are TV sets or other people who have been brought up the same way as those whom they baby sit. Many a time, baby sitters are young girls who need money for their own drugs or alcohol. They do not have any training in taking care of babies. While baby-sitting, they themselves may be smoking or taking illegal drugs. Under such circumstances, children do not receive enough necessary care, guidance, love and, most important, basic education.

No baby sitter can give the same love and care as mothers do. Children can never relate to baby sitters as they do to their own parents.

When they grow up, such children may start their own careless and misguided way of life. They don't receive proper religious education. Nor do they know how to explore religions on their own. To make things worse for them, TV violence become their role model. Many movie producers and writers are writing books promoting violence primarily so they can make a few quick dollars. Children who grow up without proper guidance lay their hands on these books and try to imitate what they watch on TV and what they read in books.

Many parents are also not very careful about their guns and alcohol. Some parents drink and smoke in front of their children. When they lose their sense of responsibility under the influence of alcohol, their senses are so dulled that they do not remember to put away their bottles, cigarettes and guns in appropriate places or to hide them away from children. They also unmindfully and carelessly keep their loaded guns accessible to children. Children are inadvertently encouraged to satisfy their natural curiosity by using guns, alcohol, drugs and cigarettes.

Some parents, who themselves come from broken families may be without enough education in morality and ethics to restrain their senses and so misbehave in front of their children. Some parents, grandparents, uncles, and brothers even sexually abuse young children. Sexually abused children grow up with unforgiving hatred towards their abusers. Sometimes they themselves can turn to similar crimes when they grow up.

Society often makes matters worse for troubled families and their children. Gun producers are very glad to see more and more people using guns to increase their income. Drug users make greater profits by using small children, mostly from broken families, for distributing and using drugs. Children who make money by selling drugs do everything to encourage their peers to use and deal in drugs. When their parents are not at home it may be even more of a thrill to get hold of some drugs and alcohol from their own parents' unlocked repositories.

Divorce has also become the norm of the day in many technologically advanced societies. The ones who suffer most from divorce are children. In their young and tender years, children need all the love and care possible from both parents. That is the age they need proper guidance and good examples as models to follow. That is the age when the mind absorbs everything quickly like a sponge. When their parents are divorced or separated prior to divorce, children become devastated and bewildered. Parents, who are struggling themselves to handle their emotions and to put their own lives together, cannot guide children in the right direction, nor can they pay all the necessary attention to children for their healthy growth. If totally neglected by parents, children seek solutions to their problems from friends, many of whom themselves come from broken families. None of them can truly help each other.

Even in homes untroubled by divorce, children may not see enough of their parents. Parents are extremely busy these days making money to provide comfortable lives for themselves and their children. Quite often they are not home because they have more than one job, to make more money. Some are not home because they have to make numerous business-related trips out of town. Some parents who may not be travelling are instead overly engaged in their work at the office. Some are such workaholics they cannot spend a minute in their waking life without doing something related to their jobs. Or, from very early in the morning they commute to work and cannot return home until late in the evening, bringing home some more work. They might go to bed very late in the evening and continue to think of their next day's work. They are busy working every waking moment of the day and busy thinking of their next day's work even while sleeping.

Asked why they are so obsessed with work, such parents might say that they have to earn and save to provide for their family. But since they always live in tension, they are always grouchy and grumpy. Grumbling, they wake up in the morning, and grumbling, they go to bed in the evening. Any tiny little thing can irritate them. They don't have any time for themselves or their children. They believe that if they earn more their children's future will be assured. But no matter how much they earn it is not enough. And some parents who have more than they need do not have time for their children because they spend more time with their friends than with their families.

When children come home from school, they often do whatever they like because there is nobody at home to supervise them. In some cases, parents pick up their children from schools on their way home from work and yet don't have time to listen to them. They like children to be seen but not to be heard. Children are afraid to talk to their parents lest they might anger them for speaking up about their problems. Children's problems may continue to grow, when they have no time to discuss them with their parents. Their peers are not in a position to give them meaningful advice.

Some parents look forward to having their children grow up and leave home as soon as possible, so they can be free to do what they wish to do. Sadly, their children may also look forward to growing up quickly to be free from their parents. In extreme cases, some misguided, impatient children even kill their parents to take possession of their property. Children wishing to achieve their independence as quickly as possible become more selfish. We know the problems. There is no close-loving relationship between parents and children. But what are the solutions?

Of course, both parents and children can be independent and still have a good relationship with one another. Relationships between parents and children have been highly valued by the Buddha. To promote these good relationships, the Buddha has advocated numerous measures. If parents fulfil their duties and responsibilities towards children and if children fulfil their responsibility toward parents, more harmonious and peaceful families can result.

People who equate money with happiness are often at the root of violent crimes. Almost all crimes are committed by people who have not been educated in moral and ethical values. If you invest all your interest, all your energy and time in making money or in sensual pleasure at the cost of your children's future, how can you expect your children to learn the distinction between good and evil? Or if you teach your children to hate your neighbor because the neighbor is different from you and your values, how can you expect your children to respect anybody?

Or if you teach your children to hate others who follow a religion different from yours, how can you expect your children not to be violent? Or if you teach your children to hate others for speaking a different language which you don't understand, how can you expect them to reduce crimes in the society? There is a low number of violent crimes in societies where there is a close family link between parents and children, a close relationship between relatives and between families. In societies where there is a free exchange of time, wealth, energy, knowledge, love and care, violent crime diminishes.

Blessed are the parents and children who have a loving relationship between them. Blessed is the home where there is friendship and harmony. Parents should make some sacrifices to give all their love and care to their children. Wise parents should invest their time, energy and money to create a healthy home environment where they can bring up their children happily. To take care of their children, some benevolent parents take turns working outside the home. In some cases, it would be advisable for parents to change their work schedules, if both must work to earn sufficient income to support their families. Sometimes, either the father or the mother may decide to stay home to take care of their children if one of them earns enough income to support the family.

Good parents should realize they are role models for their children. To discipline children, parents must be disciplined themselves. If parents are undisciplined, they cannot expect any discipline from their children. When parents do try to discipline their children, sometimes the children may rebel against them. They might even say they hate their parents. Nevertheless, good parents should not be afraid of children's comments such as these. When children grow up they will realize their parents disciplined them for their own benefit.

Sometimes, children may have an important topic, related to anxious feelings or learning problems or peer-problems, and may wish to discuss them with their parents. Then, parents must listen to them mindfully, patiently and compassionately. During the discussion, if children use abusive language parents should reprimand them immediately then allow them to continue the discussion. If they show emotion, parents should not play a co-dependent role and also become emotional, but listen mindfully, hoping to help them. In other words, when children are angry, parents should listen to them mindfully and patiently without themselves getting angry, so they can be effective in helping children.

Parents and children should have open and friendly discussions regularly. Parents should admit their mistakes and apologize to children. If parents shout, curse or throw their own temper tantrum, they should apologize to children either immediately or later on and explain the reason why they behaved that way. They should determine not to repeat that kind of behaviour in front of children. Children also should be encouraged to admit their mistakes and apologize to parents. Parents should appreciate the good things children do and acknowledge any improvement they have made. Reward and punishment works with everybody.

If there are several children in a family, parents should be equally fair to all of them. In dealing with family problems, parents always should exercise caution to do justice to all of the children. If they should praise one child more than others in front of everybody, their siblings may become jealous of the one that was praised. When parents are full of loving-kindness and compassion, solving any family problem is easy.

Parents should treat children with honour and dignity, as wonderful human beings who are going to take the world's responsibility into their hands one day.

Whenever children do something good, parents should not forget to appreciate and reward them, at least in words. When children do something unethical, immoral and harmful, parents should immediately reprimand them and talk to them directly. Parents should know when to reprimand them in private and when to reprimand them at a family meeting, in front of everybody. Also, neither the father nor mother should criticize each other in front of children. They should have their own private meeting to discuss problems.

Parents should choose the right words, right attitude, right moment and right place to tell the right things to children. In every situation parents should make sure that they really and sincerely love their children. They must assure their children that they honestly love them. If you humiliate children in front of everybody, children may do many wrong things secretly. They will also learn to be hypocritical. Parents must be very honest with children. If parents are dishonest, children lose respect for them. You as parents cannot demand respect if you don't deserve it. You should learn to earn it by your own behavior and attitude towards children. And don't expect to be their teacher all the time. Children, too can be very good teachers to parents.

'One of the best things parents can do to establish and maintain a friendly and loving relationship with children is to spend some time practising loving-kindness and meditation. They should make it a habit to encourage children to join them a few minutes every day practising meditation. In many good Buddhist families, parents and children spend a few minutes reciting some religious verses. They have little home shrines where they gather every day at least for a few minutes.'

-Ven Dr. Henepola Gunaratana, USA.

JUVENILE DELINQUENCY

Any discussion of juvenile delinquency raises two fundamental questions: (1) Who are the juveniles? and (2) What constitutes delinquency? In answer to the first question, the most common criterion employed is chronological age. The vast majority of the laws dealing with juvenile delinquency throughout the world provide an age limit beyond which special procedures and measures meant for juveniles are inapplicable. The age limit applicable to juveniles in Malaysia will be dealt with later in subsequent paragraphs.

The second question as to what constitutes delinquency is more difficult to answer. The word delinquency is derived from the Latin *deliquesce* meaning 'neglect', and it may be interpreted in broad terms as neglect on the part of juveniles to conform to the accepted standards of behaviour in a given society. An antisocial act is defined as a criminal offence constituting delinquency when committed by a juvenile.

Some of us have a black sheep in the family or in our midst. What is the cause? Research has disclosed a number of factors which show how a young child may face the danger of falling into crime. The main reasons for crimes are stated to be: (a) criminal history in the child's family; (b) unhappy family back-ground arising from inconsistent behaviour by parents where harsh and erratic discipline is mixed with generosity in the provision of material gifts; (c) large family size; (d) a record of truancy, and (e) failure to do well at school.

A juvenile delinquent probably comes from a bad home environment, has no self-confidence, no belief in his own identity and no experience of normal satisfaction. The key to the solution will be the family. To what extent are parents responsible for this state of affairs? The young persons who commit petty crimes could have been neglected in childhood. They want possessions and money. But because they do not know how to earn them they steal them. Those who commit violent crimes, in addition to having been neglected, usually are treated cruelly in childhood. They do not feel ashamed about going to prison. They have no sense of letting anybody down and they have no desire for social approval.

Divorced parents often create serious emotional problems for children. They are deprived of family traditions which could have helped them to behave with correctness and decorum.

There is no way to make children do anything once they become truly defiant. Punishment and reward have their limitations. When do we start controlling or motivating our children? Psychologists maintain that it is in the first couple of years of life that the largest part of this process takes place during which period parental love arouses the corresponding love in children.

This period is vital to guide the child

as he grows up to be a responsible or an anti-social person. In these modern times many six to seven year old children are no longer the little darlings we admired and caressed, but are often defiant little brats. Parents are largely responsible for such behaviour. We should nurture habits of serious critical thought in our children, teaching them to measure actions against consequences.

At this stage of development of children, the school has an equal responsibility with parents. Some children are afraid to go to school for fear of being bullied or teased or of being too self-conscious of their appearance or worried about doing badly in their school work or have fear of teachers. In the light of such experiences, an attempt to make the lives of children from five to six years more secure is appropriate.

Recent reports on juvenile delinquency released by the Welfare Services Department show a sharp increase in the number of criminal cases (300 per cent since 1962) committed by those below 18. This is indeed saddening, seeing how much effort has gone into programmes and projects to propagate and foster a caring society. Over 4000 juvenile delinquents were arrested in 1995, compared to about a thousand less in the previous year.

Most of the youths caught were those

who had difficulties in school. Indiscipline among students has reached an alarming stage. Teenage delinquency has been caused by the lack of attention received at home, the presence of unhealthy elements in 'shady' video game and amusement centres an mixing with bad company. The study had singled out students living in squatter areas and low cost flats as the most vulnerable and problematic.

Datuk Seri Dr. Mahathir Mohamad, the Prime Minister of Malaysia, said that if the Government closed down certain centres where people encourage young person to get into some immoral practices, they may do the same thing secretly.

Police have also expressed concern over rising gangsterism and assault cases in schools. Such criminal activities need to be curbed to prevent more pupils from getting involved in serious crimes. Headmasters and teachers should counsel and advise pupils against getting involved in criminal activities. The police should be called in only if the problem is beyond their control.

Hisham Harun writes in *The New Straits Times* dated March 5, 1997:-

'Police statistics reveal that in 1994, the number of arrests for crimes including drug addiction, rape, incest, house-break-ins and car thefts stood at 4,192. Out of this, a total 1,839 males and 23 females were Malay compared to 590 Chinese males amd 18 females. and 421 Indian males and 10 females.

The following year, the number of Malay offenders in this age group rose to 2,402 while the number of Chinese youths arrested totalled 922; 507 Indian youths were caught. Last year's figures were 2,890 Malays, 770 Chinese (registering a drop) and 574 Indians, with Selangor, Johor and Kedah posting the highest crime rates among youths in the past three years. Malay youths made up the bulk of offenders in all States.

National Unity and Social Development Ministry statistics seem to support the police figures and show that of the 2,898 juvenile cases involving drug abuse and other social problems, 61 per cent of the offenders were Malays, 17 per cent Chinese and 10 per cent Indians. In addition, Malays make up at least 70 per cent of inmates at the Hendry Gurney School for boys in Malacca.'

Sociologists and welfare officers point the finger at the pressures of modern living, which inevitably lead to a collapse of strong community and family bonds. Who then are the people who need counselling? It would appear that the parents need it as well, not just the juvenile delinquents.

Datuk Adul Kadir bin Jasin, Group editor of *The New Straits Times* stated in the *Sunday Times* in Malaysia that elders are also to be blamed for the social ills in the country.

Adolescence is often a time of conflicts – physically, emotionally and psychologicaly. It has now been established that most juvenile delinquents are school children. When school children display behaviour that merits concern, the authorities should call up their parents and make them aware of what has been observed about their children.

Such early 'warnings' could help parents take some preventive or remedial measures before their children add to the statistics of the country's criminal records. As such, the home and the schools have very important roles to play in the prevention of juvenile deliquency. If parents pay attention to the advice given by the Buddha as their duty towards their children, many of the problems created by the children can be curbed.

Running Away From Home

Running away from home is becoming a serious problem among our young people which gives parents much cause for concern. A 'runaway' youth is one who leaves home without permission with the intention of not returning. Young people run away because they feel a situation is intolerable. They see running away as a solution. But, in fact, it only takes them physically away from the problem. The mental stress and the trauma remain.

A social psychologist who has studied this modern day problem says running away 'is an irrational response to stress and frustration'. Indeed, 'there is enough reason in the home and school environments to prompt even the most mentally healthy person to consider flight as a way of coping.'

When a child starts to think about running away, he asks himself many questions. He bargains with himself a lot more than we adults think. Yet they are willing to give up the known security of home, however limited, for the unknown promises of a new environment. Why? It is because they are so desperate that they perceive that any alternative is better compared to the suffering they undergo at home. Running away is rarely well planned. It is a spontaneous, impulsive behaviour.

Some parents rigidly select and restrict their children's friends. Such parents may as a result encourage their children to think of running away – towards the promise of greater freedom outside their home. Girls tend to run away to escape a closed family and their parents' over-protectiveness; for example, having to make decisions about boy friends. Boys on the other hand often run away because they have been unsupervised for far too long. They have developed an impulsive and escapist behaviour, having got used to an unstructured life-style.

Strain may also sometimes arise from too little parenting. Parents preoccupied with work problems may be incapable of correcting their child's behaviour. On the other hand running away is almost always tied to excessive parental control and unrealistic parental expectations.

The country's current strong economic growth has led to various social problems which have affected the nation's youths.

With the advent of satellite television and the information superhighway, our youths will be exposed to even more information containing negative values which would lead to moral decay now haunting many youths in developed countries. We must prepare ourselves for the challenges of a new world ahead.

Moral Decay

Moral decay is already evident in our midst judging from the number of social problems, namely drug abuse, loitering, *bohsia* and *lepak*

culture among youths, illicit sex etc.
From a study conducted by the Youth and Sports Ministry on 5,860 youths, 71% smoke, 40% watch pornographic videos, 28% gamble, 25% consume alcohol and 14% take drugs. Eleven juveniles from various detention centres throughout the country have been identified as carriers of the Human Immunodeficiency Virus (HIV) which causes AIDS. Ten of them are in fact below 20 years of age.

The authorities are concerned about the juveniles being confirmed HIV carriers and are closely monitoring the situation. Initial checks showed some of the juveniles were not drug addicts but had been involved with them. The majority of the cases were discovered through counselling and voluntary medical tests.

This unhealthy trend can only be curbed with direct influence from parents. Parents should monitor the movements of their children to ensure that they are not involved in any immoral or illegal activities.

Without early monitoring and control, children can become easy prey to unhealthy influences. If this is allowed to continue, the teenagers will move on to more serious crimes. The emergence of various social problems must be addressed urgently. Hence parents must strengthen the family institution to withstand the demands of a changing society.

Punishment

In law, according to our Penal Code, 'Nothing is an offence which is done by a child under 10 years of age. Further, nothing is an offence which is done by a child above 10 years of age and under 12, who had not attained sufficient maturity of understanding to judge the nature and consequences of his conduct on that occasion.'

There is a conclusive and absolute presumption in law that a child below 10 is incapable of knowing right from wrong although in truth, the child could have done the forbidden act with premeditated intention.

The second category of children, those between 10 and 12, are in a 'twilight zone' in which they are exempted from criminal responsibility unless it is proven by the prosecutor that the child was of normal mental capacity with a proven mischievous tendency.

Although a child under 10 is free to do any crime and can escape punishment, he cannot totally escape all the consequences. Although there is no punishment as such his future behaviour may be restricted. The person who instigates a child to commit a crime will be charged as the principal offender, the child being treated only as an innocent agent.

The Juvenile Court is the pivot around which revolves the machinery for the treatment of juvenile delinquents. The law relating to juveniles is embodied in the Juvenile Courts Act 1947 and Children and Young Persons Act 1947. A juvenile is defined as a person aged between 10 to below 18 years.

The Juvenile Court is not open to the public. Although newspaper reporters may attend they cannot reveal particulars that may identify the offender. If found guilty, the court does not use terms such as 'convict' or 'sentence' in relation to the offender.

The court is presided over by a first class magistrate who decides on guilt. He sits with two assessors, one of whom should be a woman if possible, to assist him on deciding the 'sentence'. Before deciding how to deal with a juvenile, the court considers the offender's general conduct, home environment, school record and medical history.

The court may admonish and discharge, grant a discharge upon the offender entering a bond to be of good behaviour to comply with such orders as may be imposed, a committal to the care of a relative or other fit person, and order his parents or guardian to execute a bond to exercise proper care and guardianship, a probation order, an order of committal to an approved school or Henry Gurney School, for 'corrective' education, an order to pay a fine, compensation or costs.

Imprisonment may only be ordered if the offender is aged between 14 and 18 years. It is the last resort provided the delinquent cannot be suitably dealt with in any other way possible.

A child between 10 and 14 years cannot be ordered to be imprisoned for any offence. Neither can it be committed to prison in default of payment of a fine, damage or costs. Under Section 16 of the Juvenile Courts Act, a juvenile cannot be sentenced to death. However the restriction is not applicable where a juvenile is charged under Essential (Security Cases) Regulations 1975 which expressly excludes the Juvenile Courts Act. The only situation where an ordinary court may try a juvenile is when he is jointly charged with another adult or the offence carries the death penalty. Possibly, in such cases, the juvenile may be pardoned and committed to the Henry Gurney School.

Where a child below 10 years is intolerably mischievous or even otherwise needs care and protection being beyond the control of anyone, the Juvenile Court makes an order vesting the custody and protection of the child to an approved institution.

One of the most frequent measures of treatment applied by juvenile courts is probation. A juvenile delinquent is placed under the supervision of a probation officer whose duties are to befriend and assist him with a view to his rehabilitation. Probation is essentially social case work because it is the task of the probation officer to find regular employment for his charge and assist in his family problems whenever necessary.

The spirit behind the law relating to youngsters is that they should be treated differently from adults, that is, with compassion and understanding so that they are shown the correct path from which they strayed through no fault of their own.

The advice that could be given to families with young children is to spend quality time with them, to listen to what is going on, and what the child may be really trying to tell.

"Bohsia" and "Lepak" Culture among Youths

With rapid industrialisation of the country many youths from the rural areas flock to larger cities in search of employment in factories. Girls from the rural areas in particular come in large numbers to be employed mostly in electronic factories. The lure of a care-free life in the city with their many shopping complexes, supermarkets and bright lights attract many rural youths who generally spend their leisure hours after work indulging in 'window shopping' or merely loitering around in groups in such places. Money is uppermost in their minds – some extra cash with which they could enjoy a better quality of fashionable life in the city.

This kind of lifestyle among youths in the course of time gave rise to the popular use of the terms *bohsia* and *lepak (Bahasa Malaysia)*. The word bohsia originates from Chinese Hokkien meaning 'voiceless'. How the term originated and came to be associated with loafing youths in large cities is however obscure. Its Bahasa Malaysia equivalent is *lepak*.

With a large proportion of these teenage youths being away from the social controls of normal rural family life, it was indeed not surprising to find some of them indulging in unwholesome activities in large cities and becoming involved in a way of life which would not normally be tolerated back in their own rural home towns. Inevitably a decline in ethics set in due to the absence of the sanctions of parents and society back in their own villages.

A stage was reached when female

teenagers in small groups would place themselves a 'pick-ups' at strategic locations in shopping complexes, public buildings or street corners, only to be 'picked-up' by local youths. The girls are so naive they became easy prey to those roving romeos in super motorcycles.

One could in fact approach and strike up a casual acquaintance with any factory girl seen loitering in the vicinity of shopping complexes and the chances are that she would readily accept an invitation from such an acquaintance for a drink or snack at a restaurant and later adjourn for a walk or to a disco or any place mutually agreed upon.

Later on however, the female teenagers, having grown wiser to the scheme of things, elevate themselves to solicit acquaintance with affluent older men who would prowl around in expensive cars looking for 'pick-ups' to keep them company. These men in high society would generally be lavish in entertaining the girls. The situation in the course of time however got out of hand when cases of *khalwat* (close proximity) were apprehended by the police, who also received complaints lodged by wives against their husbands involved in vice activities. With continued action and surveillance by the police, the *bohsia* and *lepak* problems, which at one time had occupied news headlines to a large extent, gradually faded away.

To fill the void that ensued, unscrupulous business operators took the opportunity of raking in money by opening up karaoke lounges and video arcades thereby providing ideal rendezvous facilities with subdued lighting and popular music for 'boy-meets-girl' situations. Despite government regulations, karaoke and video arcades still allow children under 18 years of age to patronise their premises and their operating hours extend up to 3.00 am or 4.00 am. Both sexes mingle freely in the dimly-lit premises and their behaviour leaves much to be desired.

Karaoke centres employ attractive young ladies as 'guest relation officers' as a front to seduce youths to indulge themselves in shows where they are encouraged to spend excessive amounts of money. In video-clip shows scantily dressed men and women move around lewdly to erotic music. One could imagine how much adverse influence it could have on a young mind. Teaching moral values in school alone will not create a healthy society. Parents too have to weed out negative elements, and the media needs also to play a positive role in this regard. Society has to nip the festering problem in the bud by disallowing the young mind to be poisoned by such lewd video shows.

There is a move by the Government to clamp down on karaoke lounges and video arcade centres as this will help to curb social ills prevalent among youths. Many such centres operate under disguise as their main activities are gambling and drug peddling. Their activities are highly computerised and, using remote control, they can quickly re-set the games when raids are carried out on the premises. This has made it difficult for the police to take action against them unless they go undercover. The Police are aware of criminal activities taking place in video, amusement and karaoke outlets.

We want to strengthen family ties and promote healthy family values. We do not want our youths to spend their leisure time and money in karaoke and video outlets as this could lead them astray. By closing video and karaoke outlets youths would be less likely to waste their time and this would encourage them to engage in wholesome activities or stay at home with their families.

In the *Sigalovada Sutta* the Buddha has given advice to youths not to mingle during unusual times in the streets and certain places where people can influence young people into immoral practices.

THE PROBLEM OF DRUG ABUSE

During the early 1960s, the 'hippie' subculture swept the West making a deep impact on human civilization. A typical 'hippie' was seen as a young unkempt person wearing gaudy coloured casual clothes and long hair, advocating freedom of thought and expression, and rejecting many of the conservative standards and values of society. Smoking cannabis (ganja) was their favourite form of drug abuse. Our local youths copied this lifestyle to a certain extent. Although with hindsight we can say that the hippie movement did have some positive effects, its permissiveness paved the way for the greatest scourge mankind has ever known: drug abuse.

When drugs are abused, the results can be devastating — for the abuser, for those who care about him or her, and for society at large. Dependence on commonly abused drugs has become one of the leading public health problems. The escalating drug toll is quite unacceptable, in terms of wasted lives, destabilised families, and rising crime rates, quite apart from the high costs of funding research programmes, rehabilitation centres and specialised law-enforcement agencies. The severe harm addiction causes the human body and the difficulty of overcoming the problem are beyond doubt.

Repeated use of drugs can cause the user to become dependent on them. Physical dependence on a drug like heroin for example, is characterised by increasing tolerance to the drug – that is, the user has to take ever larger doses in order to achieve the same degree of drug – induced euphoria, or 'high'. And this of course makes the withdrawal symptoms, (the often severe physical reactions the user may experience when denied the drug) much worse. Traditionally, drug addiction has been defined as physical dependence. Today the term drug addiction usually refers to a behavioural pattern marked by compulsive use of a drug and a preoccupation with getting it.

Drug abuse has been rated as one of the world's greatest enemies. Society has ascribed the cause of this scourge to the moral degradation of our youths who have strayed from their normal family home environment to be enticed by influences outside the home. Many use drugs as a means to escape from unhappy home situations. Parents who are too busy to attend to the social and spiritual needs of their adolescent children often neglect them to the extent of driving them to seek solace in drug addiction. The lack of proper parental guidance and supervision and the low regard for values of life, such as morality and spirituality has to a large extent contributed to this negative state of affairs. Many addicts began with no intention whatsoever of becoming addicted but they were sadly mistaken when they became enslaved to the habit.

It is significant to note that drug trafficking has even surpassed international oil trading as a money spinner and is second only to the arms trade. The lucrative trade in drugs has made its distribution widespread and caused serious socio-economic problems in both developed and developing nations. Drug traffickers are in fact known to be using complex corporate structures and dealing in intricate business transactions involving banks, trust companies, financial institutions and real estate firms.

Drug abusers invariably progress on to hard drugs and 'mainliners' live under the perpetual threat of an overdose. The common habit of sharing needles to 'fix' or inject drugs into one's body system by hard-core 'mainliners' is one of the principal causes of the spread of AIDS now threatening the country, which will be discussed in detail in the next section.

The Government is currently spending millions of dollars on various drug rehabilitation programmes as the ever growing problem of drug abuse by our youths is increasing to alarming proportions.

It is significant to note that infants born to heroin-addicted mothers also become addicts. Because the mother's heroin intoxication can penetrate the placenta barrier (the buffer between her bloodstream and that of the foetus) and pass directly on to the unborn child, doctors try to find out beforehand if a mother is on heroin (many would not admit it) so that the child can be treated and handled as an addict from the moment it is born. If a doctor is unaware of the mother's addiction problem, the new born baby may go into an immediate and life-threatening withdrawal state. This can include breathing problems, convulsions and trembling.

According to reports a vast majority (98.8%) of addicts are men, with more than 80% of them aged between 20 and 39 years. More than 41% of addicts caught the habit because of peer pressure, 36.8% were seeking pleasure on their own initiative while 15.6% took drugs out of curiosity. Others became addicted to overcome mental stress (4.6%), as a result of medical treatment (1%), by accident (0.4%) and 0.1% as a sexual stimulant.

How can parents tell if their children in the adolescent age group (12 to 21 years) are on drugs? Millions of parents are quite rightly concerned about this problem and worry about the appeal of drugs to youngsters. What they are obviously concerned about is illicit drug use. Your suspicions that one of your children is involved in drug-taking may be aroused by an unexpected change in his or her behaviour patterns. He or she may appear confused, have slurred speech, become aggressive, paranoid or depressed, suffer weight loss, display red eyes, drowsiness, reveal declining performance at school etc. If faced with irrefutable evidence, it is best not to over dramatise the situation but to get the help of trained counsellors who will best know how to handle the situation. The worst action would be to deny that the problem exists.

One of the best ways to help your child avoid drugs is to set a responsible pattern at home – do not abuse potentially addictive products, such as alcohol or tobacco, yourself. If you find that your child is involved, do not confront him while he is affected. Instead approach him later and try to discuss the problem and any underlying adolescent difficulties that may relate to it.

There are two major aims to bear in mind: to keep on good terms with the child, who will often be the only person able to tell you what is going on, and to establish some firm facts about the drug used – whether smoked, swallowed, injected or inhaled, also how long and how often it has been taken. You should then consult your family doctor, who will advise you on the most sensible policy to adopt. If the situation is serious your doctor may refer you to a rehabilitation centre or to a hospital.

THE SPREAD OF AIDS

AIDS (Acquired Immune Deficiency Syndrome) is now the most deadly of all sexually transmitted diseases. AIDS is caused by the human immunodeficiency virus (HIV), which attacks and weakens the body's immune system so that it can no longer fight off infections normally controlled with ease. A person with AIDS is not likely to survive, although it is not the actual AIDS virus which kills him. The cause of death may be any of the wide variety of organisms that can enter the body and, finding little resistance, multiply wildly. The victim is thus subject to a variety of rare illnesses normally found only in a relatively mild form if they do occur, in people with a normal immune system.

People who have AIDS die from a secondary disease. The two illnesses most commonly identified in AIDS patients are pneumonia and a rare form of skin cancer, as a result of the breakdown of the body's immune system.

Once the virus enters the body, it is targeted to attack the immune system of the human body. The AIDS virus is carried in the body fluids, particularly blood and semen, of people who suffer the disease. Persons so infected can transfer the virus to their sexual partners or spread it by contaminated blood during transfusions. An AIDS infected mother can transmit the deadly virus to her child, during or shortly after birth.

The AIDS virus also circulates in the blood of its victims. This is almost certainly why intravenous drug users and haemophiliacs are in the higher-risk group. Intravenous drug users often share needles, and a needle used by an AIDS carrier can transmit the needle used to anyone who uses the same needle. Since many people donate blood to blood banks, it is possible that AIDS-contaminated blood might be given to a haemophiliac, and indeed some people have been infected by this way. It is almost impossible, of course, to get AIDS by donating blood, since the needles used for the procedure are sterile and are discarded after each use.

The inherent danger of the deadly disease is that AIDS antibodies, which indicate infection, only appear in the blood a few weeks, and sometimes a few months after the person has been infected. The incubation period however, varies greatly and can be quite long, perhaps as long as five years. Hence it is not possible to detect infection immediately after exposure. With no known cure or vaccine so far, AIDS prevention is indeed most vital.

The following symptoms occur in AIDS : swollen lymph nodes, recurring fevers, night sweats, sudden unexplainable weight loss, fatigue, diarrhoea, purplish skin lesions and unusual infections.

The results of several investigations into the spread of AIDS indicate that people living in the same house, sharing eating utensils, or being exposed to sneezes from an infected person do not become infected with AIDS virus. Nor is it possible to be infected from swimming pools, handshaking or sharing toilet seats. The only known routes of infection are sexual contact and exposure to contaminated needles or blood.

Nearly half a million people around the world are officially reported to have AIDS. This is just a third of the estimated total of eleven million people carrying the potentially lethal virus HIV.

The global total of carriers is estimated to be 446,681 spread over 163 countries. In our country alone, the known number of HIV carriers has reached more than 2,500 and 31 of the 37 AIDS victims have died. By the year 2000, it is estimated that more than 60,000 infants will have AIDS, and 120,000 children will become orphans !

There has been a 440% increase in HIV /AIDS cases over the last five years. Data compiled by UNAIDS prove the gravity of our situation.

The country's AIDS strategy is a plan on AIDS prevention that is based on proper morals. The plan will 'go back to the basics', that is, religion, cultural and traditional values, as today's teens are indulging in activities their forefathers would never have dreamt of doing in their day. The danger of sexual misconduct is explained in the teaching of the Buddha.

ADDICTION TO TOBACCO SMOKING

Tobacco smoking covers a wide range of nicotine–laden products and includes cigarettes, cigars and pipe smoking. Of the above mentioned categories, cigarette smoking is the most prevalent. It has been established statistically that nicotine addiction usually starts among the young, and smokers are usually hooked to the habit by the time they become adults. 'Catch 'em young, and you have 'em for life' seems to be the corporate strategy of the tobacco industry.

Right now, Malaysia seems to be in a tobacco 'cloud-nine' oblivion. Our sports events, youth rock concerts, film shows and trendy holiday programmes are sponsored by tobacco companies. They advertise themselves on TV, radio and in the print media in a very subtle way by promoting products and services totally unrelated to their trade. Although their esteemed end product — the all-important cigarette, appears nowhere in sight, the message and logo they want to put across to the public nevertheless ring loud and clear. Despite public criticism, our authorities continue to allow such brand names and logo promotions as well as free distribution of cigarette samples at rock concerts.

Whatever has happened to our laws on anti-smoking, and who are enforcing them? Are they to be observed only within the vicinity of hospitals, the courts, gas stations and certain public buildings? Even the Congress passed Bills recently defining nicotine as an addictive substance. Now that the vast US market is rapidly being closed to tobacco companies, we can expect a more aggressive and well-planned campaign upon the youth in Third World countries. Malaysia, an economic success story, is certain to be a 'prime target'. Are we ready for this onslaught upon our youngsters in this country? This pandering to cigarette traders must come to an end. Or else, are we admitting that U.S President Clinton cares more for his American youngsters than we care for ours.

Malaysia as a responsible nation should unite to protect the health of our next generation. Government agencies, the corporate sector and local Non-Government Organisations (NGO's) should work together on a single policy to thwart the insidious strategy of the international cigarette companies. The authorities should lay down single-minded policies and detailed plans to curb smoking among youths. Cigarette companies are required by law to print a warning notice on all cigarette cartons about the dangers relating to smoking but, as could be expected, this usually appears in almost microscopic print, merely to conform with official policy.

Cigarette smoking is one of the contributory causes of heart disease which is already a major killer in this country and its medical and social costs are growing each year. We cannot afford to allow the tobacco habit to destroy the health of our younger generation; hence we must act now, and as one society.

There is no such thing as a 'safe' cigarette. Low-tar, low nicotine cigarettes, according to manufacturers' tests, provide some risk reduction as far as contracting lung cancer and heart disease is concerned. These tests, however, are performed on smoking machines and not on human beings. In addition, switching to a low nicotine brand is not a reliable alternative to quitting, especially for those who increase the number of cigarettes they smoke to maintain former nicotine levels.

Even though you do not inhale when smoking, you are still holding the smoke in your mouth and thus increase the risks of developing oral cancer. In addition, you may be inhaling some smoke without being aware of it, and you are breathing in glycoprotein (a tobacco ingredient that may cause some damage to the blood vessels) both during the time you are actually smoking each cigarette and for a while afterwards.

If you can stop smoking instantly, and find that you don't experience an intense craving for tobacco or such signs of withdrawal as nervousness and headaches, then you would not be classified as addicted. But the chances are that you probably would not be able to give up without feeling some symptoms, in which case you would be described, and accurately so, as addicted.

It is never too late to stop smoking,

even after 25 years. Quitting offers both short and long-term benefits. You will soon notice some changes once you have given up smoking. You will be able to taste food better and breathe more efficiently and your 'smoker's cough' will clear up. Although your lungs will never return to the state they were in before you took up smoking, some of the damage may clear up. The good news, of course, is that if you quit smoking your lungs will cease deteriorating further.

Before heart surgery doctors may ask whether the patient used to smoke or not. If the answer is 'yes', they will delay the operation to clean the lungs of 'tar' accumulated in the lungs of the smoker.

Many smokers do gain weight when they quit. But the good news is that these people gain an average of only two to three kilograms. Should you want to avoid weight gain, make quitting smoking your first priority. Remember the enormous health benefits of quitting smoking, and do not allow your worries about gaining weight to get in the way. You can work on reducing weight after quitting smoking, as a second priority.

The question often asked is: 'Can the smoke from other people's cigarettes harm me?' Yes, it can. The scientific evidence concerning the dangerous effects of passive smoking (inhaling the smoke of others) on people who live with or work near smokers is growing rapidly. Scientists have found a significantly higher incidence of respiratory diseases among children whose parents smoke. Other studies have shown passive smoking can cause decreased airway function in otherwise healthy adults and children. It has been reported that the harmful constituents of inhaling cigarette smoke are found in passive smoke, sometimes even to a greater extent than in inhaled smoke, and that non-smokers do indeed draw these dangerous elements into their lungs when they breathe in the smoke of others.

ALCOHOLISM

Alcoholism is a chronic illness which manifests itself as a disorder of behaviour. It is characterised by the repeated drinking of alcoholic beverages, to an extent that exceeds customary social customs.

The term 'alcoholic' is hard to define exactly since people have different reactions to alcohol and the way they use it. It usually takes 10 to 15 years of drinking five or more drinks a day (less for women) for a person to develop what might be called the full alcohol syndrome — that is, a state of physical dependence with serious damage to health and social relationships. In essence, alcoholism is not measured by the amount of alcohol consumed but rather by the way a person uses alcohol to deal with life's problems, and its effects on one's physical well-being.

Chronic alcohol abuse can damage all vital organs in the body. To begin with, it can damage the muscle cells of the heart and lead to heart failure and death. As alcohol is broken down in the liver, whose chief function is to neutralise and remove certain toxic compounds, this organ is the most vulnerable to alcohol's harmful effects.

Alcoholism can cause the liver to enlarge, become inflamed, and eventually develop the often fatal scarring called cirrhosis. One of alcohol's most damaging effects is on the brain. Abuse may lead to brain damage and mental disorders.

Alcohol taken in the early months of pregnancy can damage the heart of an unborn baby. Pregnant women who drink run the risk of causing a variety of abnormalities to develop in their unborn children (foetal alcohol syndrome).

Tolerance to alcohol means that the body chemistry has gradually adjusted to the presence of the beverage. As a result, it takes more of the substance to achieve the same response. This is why a person who drinks only rarely may become drunk just on a glass of wine. Tolerance, in fact, is one of the two key signs of dependence on alcohol. The other is the development of withdrawal symptoms when the user stops taking alcoholic drinks. The ability to drink a lot depends on several factors, such as the drinker's weight and chemistry, his physical and mental state, the length of time he has been drinking and the amount of food he has in his stomach while drinking.

Certain organisations, as part of their social gatherings, encourage their youths to participate in beer-drinking contests with offers of attractive prizes to the winners. Such organisations in doing so are unwittingly initiating innocent youths, many of whom have never taken any form of alcoholic drink, into the growing ranks of alcoholics, which eventually will lead to all sorts of social and domestic problems to their families and the community in general.

Could a person die from drinking too much at one time ? Although rare, such deaths do occur, usually as the result of drinking contests. This is because during such events as much as a large tumbler or more of alcoholic beverage may be consumed at one go. Such a massive quantity of alcohol can depress the respiratory system and, in combination with vomiting, lead to death by suffocation. In addition, it can reduce the body's production of glucose and cause a coma. Alcohol also can reduce the pain threshold and weaken the blood's clotting capacities.

The last of the Five Precepts in Buddhism advocates total abstinence from the consumption of intoxicants. The strict observance by Buddhists of this precept is extremely important for the well-being of one's mental and physical health, as disregard for the precept itself undermines the value of all the other precepts.

In winding up cocktail parties and drink sessions, the common habit among guests and patrons of having the extra 'one for the road' should be discouraged at all costs. Government's current 'don't drink and drive' policy is indeed commendable and should be strictly adhered to for the safety of all road users.

Pubs have mushroomed all over towns and are luring our youths to indulge in the drinking habit. Certain undesirable shows are known to take place in pubs and discos contrary to the licences issued to such establishments exposing them to the risk of the premises being raided by the police.

For persons in the lower rungs of the social scale, toddy provides the much needed solace for them to relax. Quite a number of them however imbibe the brew in excess, and as a result become drunk and boisterous thus creating domestic violence at home. Many from the low income group also indulge in drinking samsu distilled from rice. But what worries the authorities is the consumption of cheap illicit samsu (distilled under most unhygienic conditions) by unwary drinkers, leading to many cases of deaths that had occurred arising from drinking such toxic brews.

Alcoholics Anonymous is a self-help group of dedicated volunteers who help alcohol abusers to break their habits and offer therapy where necessary. They offer their services round the clock and can be contacted by telephone.

THE GENERATION GAP

The word 'generation' is popularly used as a measure of time, and usually represents about a span of 30 years, the period which man requires to attain maturity, and the age at which, as a general rule, the first child is born. The intervening wide gap between one or more generations is often generally referred to as the generation gap.

As could be expected, persons from different generations differ considerably in their ways of thinking, attitudes, life styles and values and hence do not see eye to eye with each other on most matters. Due to the disparity in the ages, the elderly group tend to hold set views which run contrary to the way of thinking of the younger generation. Differences of opinion will arise and this will lead to misunderstanding within the family.

Age old traditions, outmoded customs and sectarian attitudes of the elders often come in conflict with the aspirations of the youths. The younger generation of youths are made to stand critically at cross-roads at such a great moment in their inexperienced young lives. They are quite naturally averse to interference from elders and unyielding to patronising moods.

Some elderly people cannot tolerate the modern ideas and ways of living of the younger generation. They expect their children to follow the same age-old customs and traditions of their forefathers. Instead of adopting such an attitude, they should allow the children to move with the times if such activities are harmless and beneficial to progress. Elders should call to mind how their own parents had objected to certain popular modes of behaviour prevalent at the time when they were young. For example, in the '60s it was considered shocking for young people to imitate the Beatles and the hippies. Those young people have grown up and are in turn shocked by their own children's imitation of 'punk' and 'grunge'.

These differences in perception between the conservative parents and the younger generation is a common source of conflict within families of today. This does not mean that parents should hesitate to counsel and guide their children if they have gone astray due to some erroneous values.

But when correcting them, they should observe the principle that prevention is better than punishment. Parents should also explain to their children why they disapprove or approve of certain values. We know that what we call 'Asian Values' are good, but only if they are relevant to modern needs and can be adapted to suit the present situation.

A lack of proper understanding between parents and their children is actually causing them to distance themselves from each other. There should be more room provided for the children to grow and to engage themselves in better communication with their parents.

The following impassioned plea by a

teenager seeking his parents' understanding of his problems, as narrated by the youngster, would be typical in many families today.

'I have been with my parents for nearly 20 years now. I love them, but I do have problems with them. There are misunderstandings between the three of us, and the problems seem to be increasing.

These problems stem from my actions which my parents do not understand. They do not seem to understand the reasons behind what I say and do. I have tried to correct and smoothen out the ruffles between us, but to no avail.

My parents were always there for me when I was young, or whenever I needed a shoulder to cry on. So I did not mind them telling me what to do and I thought they were the greatest people on earth.

My view of things eventually began to differ from theirs, but I kept quiet since I feared retribution from them. The problems began when I was old enough to voice my opinions.

Now, I talk back to my parents, not because I want to rebel against them but because I can think for myself. I don't claim to know everything my parents know, but I can look out for myself. I will ask for help when I need it, but whether I want to heed their advice is a different matter.

My parents still see me as a child, one who needs constant supervision. I appreciate that my parents look after me, but they should give me some room and not smother me. They never hear what I say and then they tell me that I do not understand them.

They also encroach on my personal freedom as they do not understand me. Since they always watch me, I do not get any freedom to see my friends or do the things I want to do.

My parents always question my motives, but they never listen to my reasons because they never want to talk with me. Naturally, I turn to my friends and this surprises my parents.

I don't want to hurt my parents by not listening to them, but it works both ways. How can I take advice from them when they do not bother to find out the true facts? I am young, but how will I ever learn if I am not given the chance?

The problems I am experiencing originate from my parents and me. They just command me and do not give me a chance to ask them questions. In such an intolerable and stifling home situation, who then is to blame if I have to seek solace outside home with shady companions and indulge myself in negative activities? Do I have an option?

My parents could understand me better if only they took the time to speak with me and see my point of view. My parents and I must work together to solve this problem for the sake of a better home environment.'

The appearance of a generation in the 1950s which had become incomprehensible to its elders now looks far less mysterious than it did at that time of great changes in world civilization. Then, the talk was all of 'generation gap', a new phenomenon. Young people did not pass directly from school into lifelong work, and often manual labour, but had leisure, money and time to spend on themselves. A whole culture grew around them.

The inability of the old to understand the young, the belief by the young that youth will last for ever, their resistance to accept mortality — these things exist in all human societies at all times.

The generation gap, with its dramas, its heroes and its stubbornnes has become far more complex and complicated. It is now accepted as normal in the West that most people have little social contact with anyone but their own age groups. The initially benign, or at least apparently harmless, element in the fostering of differences between the generations now threatens to turn into something far darker and more menacing. The 'gap', as it is, is widening to a point of becoming a 'chasm'.

A major problem confronting many rich Western societies – Germany; the United Kingdom, Japan, Italy, Spain, among them – is that their populations have failed to replenish themselves, so that the numbers of old people are fast becoming a burden today.

Part of the promotion of a detached, self-conscious younger generation in the 1950s and 1960s represented a contempt for the old, at the very least, a discarding of wisdom, a rejection of experience, a degradation of traditional relationships between young and old.

These fostered misunderstandings, barriers between young and old, will eventually create deeper conflicts in the future. Indeed outrages by children against the old are already a serious issue in many parts of the world. Such incidents, will certainly increase with time, because of the aged, kept alive by technological miracles, by super drugs, by all the apparatus which permit life expectancy to increase. Quality of life however does not improve with the increase of population, and that's where the problem lies.

It is not difficult to anticipate just what forms of vengeful retaliation will occur when the young realise that they are expected to look after the 'surplus' population of those they regard as useless, the discarded, the ill-adapted, unproductive and the infirm. These are burdens society is increasingly reluctant to shoulder. One can imagine, therefore the arguments in favour of euthanasia gaining ground and the practice being increasingly accepted.

The problem of demography which once focused upon too many babies in the Third World, is likely to shift to those who refuse to die particularly in the developed world. Already the old say they have lived too long. They may have to be helped to remove themselves to make way for the next generation.May the Old and Young bridge the gap in the cause of Love and Understanding!

Listen to the Elders

It is not necessary to have personal experience in certain things to understand whether they are good or bad. Here is a an analogy for you to understand this situation. A shoal of fishes come across an obstruction in the water with an unusually small opening. It is actually a trap laid by a fisherman to catch the fish. Some fish want to go inside the fence and see what it is, but the more experienced fish advise them not to do so because it must be a dangerous trap. The young fish asks, 'How do we know whether it is dangerous or not? We must go in and see, only then can we understand what it is.' So some of them go in and get caught in the trap.

We must be prepared to accept the advice given by wise men like the Buddha who is enlightened. Of course the Buddha himself has said that we must not accept his teachings blindly. At the same time we can listen to some wise ones or other religious teachers. This is simply because their experience is more advanced than our limited knowledge regarding our worldly lives.

Parents usually advise their children to do certain things and not others. By neglecting the advice given by the elders, young people do many things according to their own way of thinking. Eventually when they get into trouble, they remember the elders and religious teachers and seek their help and sometimes even ask the religious teachers to pray for them.

Only then do they remember religion and seek some blessing and guidance. But they do not think the main purpose of a religion is to help us to follow certain noble principles to avoid many of our problems before they confront us. Early religious education trains the mind to cultivate the universal principles which support our way of life to live peacefully.

Can We Change
Others Without Changing Ourselves

Man by nature is gifted with intelligence. From childhood to adolescence his perception of life would be one of youthful vigour with lofty ideals and aspirations. As he reaches manhood, the age of reason dawns on him, and with his mature outlook, he soon realises that his utopian ideals held by him during his youth would have to be cast aside, and that he would have to perceive life afresh in its true perspective. With advancing age, and with mellowed outlook in life, he finds he has to change and adjust his lifestyle accordingly. Even his lofty ambitions in life held eminently by him in his younger days, will eventually have to come to terms with the realities of change. Such is the inevitable life cycle affecting Man and his ambitions.

'When I was young I set out to change the world.

When I grew older I perceived that this was too ambitious, so I set out to change my state.

This too, I realised as I grew older, was too ambitious, so I set out to change my town.

When I realised that I could not do

even this, I tried to change my family.

Now, as an old man I know that I should have started by changing myself.

If I had started with myself, maybe then I would have succeeded in changing my family, the town, or even the state and who knows, maybe the world.'

The most intelligent man and the real stupid man both do not agree to change the mind. (Confucius)

Experience Comes With Age

Through the academic knowledge that people gain without personal experience, some young people think they can solve all their problems. Science can provide the material things to solve our problems, but it cannot help us to solve many of our life's problems. There is no substitute for wise people who have experienced the world. Think about this saying, ' When I was 18, I thought what a fool my father was. Now that I am 28, I am surprised how much the old man has learned in 10 years!'

Actually, it is not the father who has learned, rather it is the youth who has learned to see things in a mature way.

More than two thousand years ago the Buddha, Confucius, Lao Tze and many other religious teachers gave us wonderful advice.

This advice can never become out-of-date being based on truth and will remain fresh forever. It is impossible to overcome our human problems by ignoring the ancient wisdom. This wisdom is to develop human dignity, understanding, peace and happiness.

Caring for Aged Parents

As parents age, it is inevitable that their bodies will gradually weaken and deteriorate in a variety of ways, making them increasingly susceptible to physical illnesses that can affect every organ in their system. As the realisation grows that there is no escape, the aging individual must try to find some way to come to terms with the disturbing new reality.

Filial piety is an important factor in caring for the aged in our traditional Asian society. As Asians it has long been the norm for us to accommodate and nurse the aged parents in our own homes as far as possible.

Do children owe any legal liability to care for old and disabled parents? Unfortunately the answer is 'No'. Parents simply have to depend on the goodwill of their children. Although we are proud about our values, and cultural heritage, unfortunately the number of elderly citizens with no savings and abandoned by their families is growing in Asia. The problem for us to consider is whether our values, including filial devotion and reciprocal love for children are being eroded because of a breakdown in traditional family relations and a changed economic and demographic profile.

Cramped flats and squatter houses are not places which are conducive to the accommodation of aged parents. There have been numerous cases in which old people have been neglected by their children or their relatives. This is a sad situation where good values and traditions are no longer practised.

Welfare homes and their environment for the most part are also not places which are conducive to the accommodation of aged parents. Of all living alternatives, placement in an Old Folks Home is without doubt the most sensitive issue often provoking guilt through self accusations of ingratitude, lack of devotion or filial piety and abandonment.

A nursing home, although somewhat expensive, offers the most satisfactory alternative. Each person must decide for himself and understand that there are no perfect choices. While long term institutionalization is a painful issue, it is essential to provide appropriate care for a debilitated parent.

Placement in a nursing facility does not mean 'putting your aged parent away', or at least it shouldn't. Family involvement remains essential for proper care, from the first step of choosing the facility, to maintaining an ongoing relationship with the staff, to regularly visiting the parent and involving him or her in family matters. They need cheering up and to know that there are people who really care for them.

Certain irresponsible persons with ill or aged parents get them admitted into third class wards of hospitals, leaving false addresses and just disappear from the scene. This indeed is a most cruel way of disposing of one's own aged parents.

A caring attitude as well as concern for the aged parents must prevail if the older generation is not to be adversely affected by the rapid socio-economic changes of urbanisation and industrialisation. It has to be realised that the aged are more affected by these changes and the degradation of moral values in society. It should also encompass the responsible manner in which the elderly are treated, cared for, respected and honoured.

This aspect of caring for the aged parents requires collective responsibility. It will also instil respect for the elderly as there is no better institution to care for the aged parents other than the family itself.

In many discourses the Buddha has advised children to pay special attention to father and mother. There is an old adage which says: 'Take good care of your parents for you will never know how much you miss them when they are gone.'

GAMBLING

Gambling is the wagering of money or other valuables on the outcome of a game, race, contest or other event. Although few societies in general have ever wholly approved of gambling, none has been able to eradicate it.

The hope of making quick money easily is what gives gambling its appeal. If the appeal of gambling is winning money, the thrill of it is in the risk that the wager may be lost. For many people gambling becomes an addiction.

The games most closely associated with gambling involve a heavy element of chance. Whereas poker, for instance, requires skill to play well, the outcome of the game is determined primarily by the distribution of the cards. Many casino games, such as roulette are dictated solely by chance. Betting on the outcome of sporting events, especially on horse racing, or on a lottery is perhaps the most widespread legal form of gambling, and in many countries, governments have created systems to funnel through legal channels the vast amounts wagered, retaining a certain proportion for their own use. Football pools are popular particularly in the West.

Gambling is not confined to any economic or social stratum. Many housewives are known to be compulsive gamblers who often neglect their family obligations and their children when they become so engrossed in the vicious gambling habit. They even gamble away their market provision money and become easy prey to loan sharks who are ever ready to come to the 'rescue' of such unfortunate women. Compulsive women gamblers are prepared even to go the extent of compromising their modesty to these human vultures in order to redeem their losses. Compulsive gambling is recognised as a sickness, and such organisations as Gamblers Anonymous exist for the purpose of helping individuals suffering from the problem.

Illegal gambling constitutes one of the largest 'businesses' in existence, and its 'gross' has been estimated to exceed that of its legal counterpart. Gambling can become the cause of the downfall of a person if he or she is addicted to it says the Buddha.

Indebtedness

Many who become addicted to gambling and liquor also become indebted in order to sustain their gambling and drinking habits and in so doing easily fall into the clutches of unscrupulous money lenders and loan sharks.

Money lenders often charge a high rate of interest on loans borrowed by debtors. Although the amount of loan advanced is low, their *modus operandi* is to make the borrower sign for a larger amount, as a form of security, In case of default by the borrower, the money lender will invariably sue the borrower through court proceedings, tendering the borrower's signed document for the larger amount as the basis of their claim.

Licensed money lenders and loan sharks are the bane of helpless alcoholics and gamblers as they often exploit the inherent human weakness of their victims. 'A drunkard's mouth dries up his pocket' – so the adage goes.

Even people in an affluent society resort to money lenders as a means of alleviating themselves from tight financial situations. Valuable properties and lands are sometimes mortgaged to these money lenders as a form of collateral in order to secure a loan for a business venture. Should the borrowers default, these unscrupulous money lenders will have no qualms whatsoever in resorting to court action to foreclose their claims. The law provides for the seizure of the debtor's property to pay the sum owed, plus the legal costs incurred. One who is not indebted to anybody experiences happiness in this life time says the Buddha.

Many heavily indebted businessmen, finding themselves insolvent, have no other option than to declare themselves bankrupt.

COMMON PROBLEMS

Human problems are complicated and entangled in various ways. From our birth up to our last breath, numerous problems confront us. It is impossible for any human being to exist without facing some sort of problems. The Buddha has advised us to understand the nature of our problems if we want to live peacefully. He has also advised us to ponder on the purpose of our existence and try to find out why we are not satisfied with our lives and the world. If we can understand this situation, there will be no reason for us to suffer from undue fear, disappointments and frustrations.

The Buddha's approach to the problems of human suffering is essentially empirical and experimental and not speculative and metaphysical.

There is no short cut for us to get rid of our problems. We must cultivate our way of life to discover the cause of the problems that we are facing. We must understand that there is no existence without any friction. If we want to be really free, we must examine our problems by reducing our egoism through understanding why these problems make life miserable.

We all like to lead very happy, contented and peaceful lives but how many of us can really experience such happiness? We are willing to do anything in everyway possible to gain satisfaction but it is very difficult to experience true satisfaction.

Superstitious Beliefs

Whenever we have problems, we approach others, and seek their advice. They may advise us to go and pray to certain gods in a temple or other places of worship or to recite certain mantras and to perform some rites and rituals.

But the Buddha's advice is entirely different. He never advises anyone to do anything without investigating the problems and analysing them to discover where the main cause of the problem is. The trouble with us is, whenever we face any problem, we suffer from fear due to ignorance and we create for ourselves unfounded fear, imagination and suspicion. After that we seek advice from others in order to get rid of them.

For example, when people face failure in their business they try to use magical power to gain good luck and success in their business. But they do not try to find out where the mistake or the weak point is and do not realise that many such practices are also based on superstitious beliefs. Some of these so-called 'seers' or astrologers exploit the ignorance of innocent people and make them believe that 'evil forces' are behind their bad luck.

The Buddha advised us to develop patience and understanding, without depending on superstitious beliefs, and to develop the rational way of life without wasting time and money on meaningless practices and also to use our own effort to overcome them in a reasonable way. Usually we cannot understand the causes of many of our problems because our way of thinking is clouded by suspicion and illusion. It is due to a lack of proper understanding that we give the wrong reasons for our problems and seek the wrong means to overcome them. We pray, we make offerings and vows by thinking that our misery is due to the working of an external force. Actually, most of our problems and worries are created by ourselves.

We do not strive to develop a correct way of life through moral and spiritual development. We think that religion is only for us to pray or perform certain rituals to get rid of our problems. If we maintain such beliefs, how can we concentrate on enriching our knowledge and understand things in their proper perspective?

The tree of civilization has its roots in moral values which most of us do not realize. Without these roots the leaves would have fallen and leave the tree a lifeless stump.

Today, we have developed our worldly life in such a way that we have no time to devote for self-discipline or to cultivate inner peace. Although we may have more than enough to satisfy our material needs like food, shelter and clothing, all the while we go on thinking of how to make more money and how to enjoy life in a worldly way even at the cost of others' rights. When we come across certain problems, we start to grumble, show our temper and create more disturbances not knowing that it is impossible to overcome our problems by adopting such an attitude.

Worries

People concentrate more on pleasure rather than on their peace and health. Some people worry by considering their future although they have more than enough at the moment. They worry about their sicknesses, old-age, death, funerals and also about heaven and hell or the next birth. Everyday they experience uncertainty in their lives. They run around searching for a remedy to end their problems. They worry when they are getting old. They worry when they cannot gain what they want. They worry when they lose their belongings or persons they love. After that, they create frustration, anguish, mental agony and suffer from mental disturbance and later these turn into physical ailments. Throughout their lives, they continue this search for peace and happiness until they die without finding the real solution.

Not knowing the real nature of life, we try to maintain it without experiencing any disappointments and changes. But life is changeable. It is a bundle of elements and energies which are always changing and the situation is always not to our satisfaction. Sometimes we feel life is not in our favour. When the elements and energies are imbalanced, we experience uneasiness, sickness, pain and many other problems. When mental energy is disturbed, we experience mental problems. After that our organs and glands also change their normal functions and affect the blood circulation, hormones, heart and brain cells.

We can avoid many of these problems if we can understand this conflict in our body and lead a natural life in harmony with natural forces which make up our physical existence.

Facing Realities

Today many people lead an artificial life not knowing its danger. Many of our problems are created by us due to our crazy attitude caused by temptation. Simplicity makes life run smoothly. Many of us realise and experience them only when we grow old.

For example, let us assume there is a pit about 100 feet deep and we put burning charcoal at the bottom. We then lower a ladder into it and ask people to go down one by one. Those who start to go down do not complain about the heat until they go further down to a depth of 30 to 40 feet. After 40 to 50 feet, they feel a certain amount of heat. When they go still further down to 70 or 80 feet and reach nearer to the burning charcoal, they will experience the sensation of burning. In the same manner, young people do not experience suffering although the Buddha says life is one of suffering. But it is a good analogy to explain that as we gain more experience we see the truth about suffering more clearly. The real meaning of suffering is experiencing unsatisfactoriness in everything.

Neighbourliness

Let us consider our families. How many families are there who live with mutual understanding and love? Here we think not only of our immediate families but also those who live around us. We can invite the whole world into our room through our T.V. but we are not willing to invite our next door neighbours into our houses to talk to them in a friendly manner. We have no time to look at the faces of our own family members but we spend many hours to see the faces of unknown people on the television screen. Even within one family we have no time to look at each other with smiling faces although we live in the same house. How can there be unity and happiness in such families? The sad fact is that this strange behaviour is very common in modern society.

Some people completely ignore their family members after their marriage. That is not the real way of life. We should maintain a community that lives by assisting each other and by giving moral support to those in need. Although they do not assist each other very often to the extent that human beings do, animals live together, sometimes protecting their group or their young from their enemies and their young always follow the elders.

It seems that today we are not living as

real human beings. We have deviated very far from our natural ways of life. That is why we have to face so many problems and hence we feel lonely. We must understand that there are some natural problems and there is no way to escape from them. There are also many other problems which are man-made, some are mind-made, resulting from illusion and ignorance or selfishness.

We are Responsible

Even educated people do not use their knowledge wisely when they come to superstitious practices that are performed in the name of religion. Try to get rid of this poor mentality by strengthening the mind and developing self-confidence. Then we can overcome many of our problems and in most cases, our imaginary problems will simply disappear.

According to some religious beliefs, there is a god who is responsible for all the good things that happen to us and if anything goes wrong, then the devil is to be blamed for it. To us it is not a very convincing belief.

Most of us simply do not try to understand why we are not happy and why we are not satisfied with our lives, and who is responsible for this situation. The Buddha teaches that we are ultimately responsible for every action of ourwhich leads to contentment or unsatisfactoriness.

Besides all major problems for which we are responsible and which affect us directly we also create some others which divide mankind and create problems such as racial arrogance, religious fanaticism, cultural and traditional discrimination, language problems, colour bar and superiority and inferiority complex by thinking the followers of other religions are their enemies and it is a sin to support the activities of another religion. They never think that the followers of every religion are trying to do some service to humanity and not do harm to others.Problems such as these indirectly contribute to our sense of discontentment.

Purpose of Religion

The purpose of religion is to guide mankind, to develop unity and a harmonious life and to cultivate humane qualities and mental purity. However, religion is being used to discriminate against other religions and to develop jealousy or hostility. Actually people are not using religion to maintain peace but to disturb and hate others. This unhealthy religious arrogance and competition have even created violence and blood-shed in many parts of the world.

At the same time, while cherishing

their own imagination or concepts as real beliefs as part of their valuable culture or traditions, some religionists ridicule the culture and traditions of others. In their beliefs and practices which they introduce as the only true religion, they promote selfish ideas for material gain, political power and self-glorification.

Manners and Customs

Manners may be defined as behaviour appropriate to living well in society. For various good reasons certain traditions have been handed down, and only very thoughtless persons would consider it worthless to follow those rules which guide us in our social relations to each other. Goethe wisely said, 'A man is really alive only when he delights in the goodwill of others'. An ancient motto, 'Manners maketh a man' still holds good even to this day.

The standards for what are considered good manners differ among people belonging to different ethnic groups and societies.

We discover the peculiarities of the manners and customs prevailing in other societies when we travel abroad. We should not prejudge other peoples' manners and custom too quickly, and decide what is proper or improper. In themselves, manners are neither good nor bad, but when they cause ill feelings in others, then this can be considered as bad manners.

We are living in an ever-changing world. We should not cling blindly to the traditions, customs, manners, rites and rituals practised by our forefathers or ancestors who adopted these practices according to beliefs and conditions prevalent during their time. Some customs or traditions handed down by our ancestors may be good, while others may be less useful. We should consider with an open mind whether these practices are congenial and relevant to the modern world.

Among members of the Chinese community emphasis is laid on continuity of the family tradition and there is great reverence for the wisdom of the elders. Ancestor worship is very ancient (dating from the second millennium BC). Life is essentially a family affair, involving prayers and offerings before tablets in the home and in ancestral temples, with an elaborate system of burial and mourning, rituals and the visiting of graves as a mark of deep respect. Ethically, their primary virtue is filial piety – an obligation to serve and honour parents and forebears without any sense of fear or gain. Such respect inevitably results in strong social solidarity within the family. Confucius, was very concerned with this reverence for the wisdom of the elders. Respect for the elders is another ancient tradition in India, China and some other countries.

On the other hand good conduct such as kindness, patience, tolerance, honesty and generosity also cannot eradicate certain problems because cunning people can take undue advantage of the good qualities of others. Therefore good qualities must be practised wisely.

Social welfare workers are trying to wipe out human problems. But their contribution also can only minimise certain problems. Some others try to settle human problems by distributing the wealth and revenue of a country equally amongst the public in so-called socialist societies. It seems that their method is also not very effective to settle human problems and has failed in many countries, since selfishness, cunningness, laziness and many other shortcomings can upset the situation.

Modern scientific education has in fact created more problems rather than promoting peace, happiness and security. Governments try to maintain peace and order by punishing those who disobey the law. But all over the world, evil and immoral practices are spreading rapidly.

Ignorant people resort to charms, magic, supernatural powers and mantras to overcome their problems. But nobody knows just how far they can succeed through such beliefs and practices.

Some use violent methods to gain what they need to settle their problems. Some others try to settle human problems by improving people's lives through financial aid.

Certain religious authorities on the other hand try to settle these problems by illustrating the concept of a paradise to create temptation and to frighten people by threatening them with hell-fire.

Whatever method people adopt to avoid their problems, they have to face more and more new problems in their day-to-day lives. The reason for this situation is that they have not realised that the main cause of most of their problems is the untrained mind and selfish desires or uncertain worldly conditions.

When we study the life of primitive people, we can see that they have to face relatively few problems. These problems are mostly related only to their need for survival. But in the so-called civilised societies of today many of our problems are due not to our desire to continue living but because we seek too much sensual pleasures. Many people believe that the purpose of their lives is only for self-gratification.

How Do We Face Problems?

We usually create some other problems while trying to solve our existing ones. If the new problem is minor, we tolerate it to the best of our ability and do what we can to alleviate the pain. For example, when we have gastric ulcers and suffer severe pain, we consult a doctor. If the doctor says that we have to undergo an operation, we will accept the fact that we will have to suffer if we want to be cured. Since we know that there is no other solution, we decide to face the new problem of the operation to get rid of the existing pain. Then we get ready to bear the pain and uneasiness during the operation thinking that we can finally be rid of the pain.

In the same manner, we are willing to tolerate certain problems or pain to overcome the existing big problem. That is why we sometimes face suffering with smiling faces. We cannot overcome our existing problems without facing some other new problems or without sacrificing something. But one thing is clear, it is impossible to settle all our problems because problems are like waves. When one wave comes down, that creates the force for another wave to go up. Sometimes a 'give and take policy' also helps to settle our problems.

The Buddha has advocated a meaningful and practical method to settle our problems. He did not recommend a method just to patch up a problem here and there simply to pander us for the time being. Rather he taught us the way to penetrate to the root of the problem and find out the main cause of it. His method was not just to reduce the symptoms of the problem like some medicines which only suppress the symptoms of the sickness but do not cure the sickness itself. If a drug or pain killer seems to act beneficially for a while in one way, it is nearly always accompanied by one or more (usually more) deleterious after effects.

When we have a severe stomach pain, or headache, we take painkiller tablets. After that, we feel better for a short while but the pain may come back. Assume that we have a very painful wound on our body. After applying all sorts of medicine, we may manage to get rid of the wound. When the doctor or somebody asks 'How do you feel now?' we say 'we feel very much better.' But can we define this word 'better'? Can we show anything to prove what that better feeling is? Here it means that there is no longer any more pain. For anything in this world, we say we feel good or nice only to tell others that there is no problem for the time being. When we say we feel 'good', we must understand that this 'good' feeling is not permanent because when the effects of the pain killer drug wears off there will be pain again. This is the nature of life. The Buddha's method for gaining permanent happiness is to uproot the main causes of the problem and not by suppressing them. Of course, some people say it is difficult to practise the Buddha's teaching, because it does not provide short-term relief. The Buddha taught that the cause of our misery is so deep-rooted that we must take strong measures to root it out permanently, so that it can never return.

To the question on how to eradicate problems, the answer given by the Buddha is 'when a wise man, established well in morality *(sila)* has developed his mind and understanding *(panna)*, then such an ardent and wise person succeeds in disentangling himself from this tangle.' A person who is diligent and understanding, by realising the real nature of existence, develops his moral behaviour or self-discipline. *Sila* means discipline of the senses, speech or action according to a moral code. When a man is diligent and wise, he knows how to face his problems and how to overcome some of them. Here the Buddha's advice for us is to be good, diligent and act wisely if we want to solve our problems. No other method can give a final solution to our problems.

Selfish Craving Creates More Problems

The modern job-oriented education system produces students who are equipped with more academic knowledge which develop selfishness. It produces clever people without any moral development. Such people do not care what happens to others or to the world so long as they alone profit on a materialistic level. Through cunningness and adopting scientific methods to achieve their selfish desires they increase their own anxieties.

Human beings are more selfish in their craving for pleasure than any other living being. They enjoy worldly lives and sensual pleasures with no thought for the welfare of others or for the survival of the species. They also like to live long to experience pleasures. They develop craving towards the property they have accumulated and are scared of death because they do not want to depart from their properties but other living beings have no such selfish ideas. They use their senses only for their survival and lead a natural life without wilfully hurting others. It has been said that only man hoards more than he can eat. All other animals take only as much as they need for their survival. What they do not need they leave alone for others. Today we even neglect our relaxation but indulge in the senses to such an extent that we have become slaves to self-gratification.

PATIENTS IN A VEGETATIVE STATE AND EUTHANASIA

What is euthanasia, one might ask? It is a word derived from two Greek words: *eu* meaning good, and *thanathos* meaning death. Put together, it means, good death.

There has been a long-standing debate on whether legalising euthanasia (where terminally ill people are allowed to commit suicide with the assistance of doctors) is murder or 'mercy killing'. The argument for legal voluntary euthanasia states that people ought to be able to die with grace, dignity and in a compassionate manner.

When a member of one's family or a relative becomes seriously ill and develops complications which result in an irreversible coma, he will invariably end up being in a 'vegetative state', or 'brain death', for the rest of his remaining life, causing much sorrow and concern to family members who will have to care and nurse him – a heavy burden indeed which will have to be borne with great courage and fortitude.

'Persistent vegetative state' is an expression which has recently come into use in the medical profession. The 'vegetative state' arises from a severe form of brain damage which results in the patient being unable to move voluntarily, speak or swallow. But he can otherwise breathe and the heart beats without assistance. If there are movements, they appear to be reflex actions rather than purposeful gestures.

As life-prolonging technology improves, society is being forced to confront a very basic question: When, exactly, does life end? While there is almost universal agreement that complete loss of brain function is equivalent to death, a debate rages among doctors and the general public alike, when it comes to patients in the persistent vegetative state (PVS).

The diagnosis of 'persistent vegetative state,' according to the Royal College of Physicians in Britain, can be made after a patient has been in an apparently 'vegetative state' for 12 months. As a description of a person suffering from this condition, 'vegetative state' is an unfortunate choice, for human beings are of an entirely different order of creation from vegetables.

The body may die but there is life after death. This belief was held even by the philosopher Plato, who had no idea of revealed religion, over two thousand years ago.

Added to the unimaginable suffering of being unable to move or communicate with their family or those caring for them, these unfortunate people have suffered the humiliation of being discussed and treated as if they were 'vegetative'. And worse, in a number of those cases, at the request of relatives, the sufferers were deprived of nutrition. The relatives described it as 'allowing them to die.' Others describe it as 'starving them to death.'

Surely there is a lesson here for all of us. Life is infinitely precious and there is no justification for taking away the life of a sick person. Indeed, we have an obligation to guard it and strive to make him or her well or, if that is not possible, at least as comfortable as we can.

There is a major distinction in principle between taking steps to end the life of a fellow human being and taking steps to eliminate or minimise pain, to give the sufferer comfort and to preserve his dignity until he breathes his last. Life is sacred and every human being is worthy of respect.

Is a person legally dead if he is in a coma and his vital organs are kept alive by an apparatus of some kind? The advanced medical technology and sophisticated procedures available in this century have posed a dilemma to many, as for instance, taking care of people in irreversible coma, commonly known as 'brain death'.

Before recent medical advances, when a patient's heart or lungs failed, his brain would also go 'dead' in no time. Similarly, when the brain failed, heart and lung failure would soon follow.

While medical opinion is more or less thus settled, the legal consequences of doctors' action or inaction in such cases remain questionable. Will they be liable to a charge of murder or manslaughter if they switch off the life-supporting machine in hopeless cases?

Euthanasia, or 'mercy killing' in crude language, is generally understood to mean the merciful act of painlessly terminating the life of a patient suffering from an incurable disease. It is legally and religiously prohibited in the case of humans. While permitting doctors to discontinue treatment, it is illegal for doctors to administer a lethal drug or injection to terminate the patient's life. It is so even though such course of action was prompted by a humanitarian desire to end the suffering.

All this does not however mean prolonging a life at any cost when it is plainly nearing its end. Allowing someone to die implies a recognition that there is some point in terminal illness when further curative treatment has no purpose and that a person in this situation should be allowed to die a natural death in peace and dignity. In no way, should this involve active or wilful destruction of someone's life. Rather, it involves a refusal to start curative treatment when no known cure is possible. While we should respect a person's wish and right to die, we need not assist him to die or commit suicide.

Where as the law considers that the discontinuance of life support may be consistent with the doctor's duty to care for his patient, it does not, for reasons of policy consider that it forms any part of his duty to give his patient a lethal injection to put him out of his agony.

The legal liability of a person who assumes responsibility for the care of another who cannot look after himself, for example, a baby or a frail person, and making the person who is in charge of the other liable for murder or manslaughter for his omission is the same as before. While we should welcome medical technology and the use of new devices such as 'miracle' drugs, organ transplants, haemodialysis machines and so on, we should guard against going down the slippery slope to the valley of euthanasia.

In disconnecting life-support machines after brain death, it is not an exaggeration to say this is a common problem for doctors and next-of-kin of the dying patient. The poser is: `Is it better for death to be accelerated in obviously hopeless cases by disconnecting the life-supporting machine?' An immediate thought occurring to mind is, how can we be absolutely sure that the case is hopeless? Miracles can and do happen, although rarely. Whether right or not, one can only safely conclude that there are many unexplained mysteries in this world. This is a matter that has been agitating the minds of the orient for many years.

Buddhism does not countenance euthanasia for two reasons. The first is that every living being has the results of its own past karma to work out, and any interference with his situation will not be anything more than a temporary alleviation of the suffering it is bound to endure. The second reason for condemning the mistaken support for euthanasia concerns the doer and the deed. The very act of killing, whatever its apparent motive, may be related to separation of life from the physical body intentionally which goes against the natural formation of life according to the following five factors: mental energy, karmic energy, germinal order, seasonal order and the order of natural phenomena. The feeling takes the form of repugnance towards suffering that is being witnessed. He disguises his real feeling as a morally praise-worthy action, and so rationalises and justifies it to himself. If he understood his own psychology better, the hidden forces of cruelty arise at the time of committing the deed.

This does not, however, prohibit the use of sedation and other therapeutic sources to allay the suffering of any person. To be able to relieve someone from suffering by any means and to create an atmosphere for healing should be considered as laudable. All those involved in the alleviation of suffering and in service of the sick should cultivate awareness in their everyday work not merely as an academic and humanitarian involvement, but also associate themselves in the truth that is a psychological process in eliminating selfishness, aversion and delusion.

Suicide

Suicide is the act of intentionally and voluntarily taking one's own life. Suicides fall into two types; conventional and personal. The first type occurs as a result of tradition and the force of public opinion. An example is *hara-kiri*, the ritualistic suicide committed by abdominal stabbing by a Japanese man of rank when he faced disgrace.

Personal suicides are more typical of modern times. The theory is generally accepted that suicide is a result of failure to adjust to one's life stresses and strains.

Suicide is a way to solve various types of personal problems – loneliness, hate, desire for revenge, fear, physical pain, feelings of guilt etc. More men commit suicide than do women, and this applies to all age groups. However, women make more unsuccessful attempts than do men, either because of lack of skill in the art of killing or because of emotional differences.

Most people who commit suicide are depressed. The highest incidence occurs in those whose depression is accompanied by a pervasive sense of hopelessness and a loss of interest or pleasure in activities. In addition, people who are older, single, divorced or widowed, and especially those who are addicted to alcohol or drugs, are at higher risk. Those who are homeless are also more serious suicide risks than others.

Teenage suicide, on the other hand, is a frightening problem. Since 1950 the suicide rate has doubled in adolescent males. For various reasons, however, a similar rise has not occurred in females.

Some experts feel that the rise in teenage suicides is due to the complexity and stress of modern life. It is also known that television dramas and news stories about suicide produce a temporary rise in the number of youngsters who take their lives. Unemployment and pressure to achieve are also factors.

There are several warning signals to watch for, including withdrawal from the company of friends and from regular activities; neglect of personal appearance; radical changes in eating and sleeping habits; and abuse of drugs and alcohol. Some teenagers make their intentions even more obvious. They may give away cherished possessions or say: 'I won't be a problem much longer'. The actual act of suicide often follows some emotional loss such as a break with a girlfriend (or boyfriend) or a family divorce.

Hence, if you should spot any of these behavioural changes – and they must be taken seriously – you should immediately discuss your child's unhappiness with him. For instance, ask specific and direct questions about what he is planning to do. Bringing things out in the open may reduce his anxiety, and he will sense your support. Only then you may be able to attack the problem itself and seek professional help if necessary.

The permissiveness of modern society, which implies greater tolerance of deviant behaviour may partly be responsible for the increase in suicidal acts, especially of self-poisoning.

Society's attitude toward suicidal behaviour has grown less moralistic and punitive. There is now a greater readiness to understand rather than to condemn, but a tendency to conceal suicidal acts still persists.

A fatal suicidal act tends to cause grief reactions and guilt feelings on the part of those who may feel that they could have prevented by caring and loving more than they did. Unsatisfied craving or failure to gain what people wanted become causes of committing suicide. No religion has ever condoned this cruel act.

The telephone is now commonly used as a means of communication among lonely and desperate individuals contemplating suicide, and seeking support and advice from members of a caring society. As in the case of 'Alcoholics Anonymous' and other similar organisations, voluntary workers serve as advisers round the clock and their services are available to would-be suicidal cases at any time. There is evidence that this kind of service does help to avert suicidal acts to a great extent.

MENTAL IMBALANCE

Mental imbalance which we regard as madness is another big problem. By violating an ethical way of life, man disturbs his own peace and happiness and that of others. Then by bringing external incidents into the mind more miseries, excitement, fear and insecurity are created.

Many people have to suffer from frustrations and nervous breakdowns because they have not trained their minds to maintain contentment. They have developed only craving for sensual pleasures. To them development means development of craving.

As a result, they also develop unhealthy competition and violence. That is how they have turned the whole world into a chaotic situation. After that, everyone cries for peace. People accuse god or the devil of putting them in misery. They do pray and worship to escape from the problems which they themselves created.

We can understand now who actually creates problems and who can overcome them. The Buddha says the world is within you. When you discipline yourself, the whole world is disciplined and peace is maintained. It is not necessary to beg for peace from others. Good and bad, peace and violence, all exist because of the trained and untrained mind.

Coping with Stress

The word stress is borrowed from physics and engineering, where it has a very precise meaning; a force of sufficient magnitude to distort or deform. In psychiatric practice however, stress involves an 'individuals' physical and emotional reaction to pressure from his environment and from within himself. There are two major types of stress; the stress involved in loss of a loved one, or a job, or of self-esteem that comes when a person's level of aspiration is impossibly high; and the stress involved in threats to the individual's status, goals, health and security. Stress gets its bad name because it may become an unavoidable part of life, and cause one to be constantly agitated. When this happens, it is possible to become overloaded and suffer physically or emotionally, or both.

Stress can be caused by any number of factors, including changes, both good and bad, personal problems, physical difficulties, illnesses etc. Common sources of stress are: death of spouse or close friend, marital separation, divorce, sexual difficulties, change of residence, child leaving home, pregnancy, in-law troubles, impending foreclosure on mortgage, dismissal (from work), redundancy, change in work responsibilities or working conditions and trouble with the boss.

Each period of one's life has its own set of stresses. In early life, the child has to cope with the immediate family group and the demands of school, adjusting to the personality of the teacher and to the other children can be very stressful, as can the problem of boy and girl relationships in later adolescence.

Then there are the academic stresses of college years and worries over career choice. After college, for most there are the problems of the first years of marriage. These can be quite serious and often lead to early divorce. The problems of having children bear heavily on women, while men have early career problems.

Some of the stress-related illnesses include peptic ulcers, migraine headaches, depression, high blood pressure, stroke and heart attacks. Continuous stress can weaken the body's immune system, and as a result the system may become less effective in battling infections. Some authorities even suggest that chronic and excessive stress may contribute to the development and progression of cancer.

In times of stress the body secretes a cascade of brain chemicals and hormones, including adrenaline and hydrocortisone, that stimulate what is known as the 'fight or flight' response. Adrenaline increases the heart rate and rate of breathing, and prepares the body to fight an external threat, or flee from it. Hydrocortisone helps to maintain its readiness for dealing with stress. Thus when we hear bad news on the phone, our immediate reaction is one triggered by adrenaline, followed by an increased secretion of hydrocortisone.

The hormones that help us to cope with stress for a short period, however, can cause health problems if we are subjected to long-term stress. Constant stress causes the body to secrete adrenaline and hydrocortisone on a continuing basis, and in time their presence in the bloodstream may be erosive. Prolonged high levels of adrenaline, for example, force the heart and lungs to work overtime and keep blood pressure above normal level. In time these changes may contribute to strokes or heart attacks.

Anxiety is the feeling of apprehension, tension or uneasiness one gets when expecting danger. We all face some anxiety in order to perform difficult tasks well, but too much can be incapacitating. Anxiety disorders constitute the most common group of mental illnesses, including the phobias, panic attacks and post-traumatic stress disorder. Many people have a simple phobia — a fear of specific objects or situations. Simple phobias are fairly common, affecting about 3% of the population.

The phobias are defined as obsessive, persistent, unrealistic, intense fears of an object or situation. Common ones are acrophobia (fear of heights); claustrophobia (fear of confined spaces); agoraphobia (fear of leaving the familiar setting of the home and being in a crowd or public place) and xenophobia (fear of strangers). They tend to avoid social situations lest they become humiliated or embarrassed. Insomnia, or difficulty in sleeping, is common in many people under many different circumstances. In fact more than 10% of people may have sleeping problems. If one is facing a temporary but important deadline at work or are under a lot of pressure, he may worry and therefore lose sleep. Our bodies prefer regular daytime activity, so shift workers have trouble adjusting their patterns of sleep.

Certain people, particularly war veterans, may suffer from what is known as post-traumatic events during the war such as explosions following artillery bombardment (shell-shock) and combat exposure, and often develop such long-term stress reactions. And the symptoms may appear or intensify long after the trauma had passed. One would experience recurrent, troubling thoughts, memories and frightening dreams or nightmares. One could be excessively irritable or anxious and may startle easily. At times he may seem to withdraw, lose interest in things he usually enjoys and feel detached from others.

The best thing one can do to cope with stress or stressful situations in daily life are perhaps obvious, but nevertheless important: eat a balanced diet, get enough sleep, exercise every day and take time to do the things you enjoy. Do not smoke or abuse alcohol or other drugs. People who are easily upset and acutely sensitive to stress can try to reduce their reactions by learning relaxation, meditation and behaviour modification techniques.

MENTAL ENERGY MUST BE TRAINED

The extraordinary mental energy or intelligence that human beings experience cannot be found in other living beings. However this mental energy is wild and free and it must be trained and controlled for us to benefit from it. Otherwise, that mind becomes the main cause of our own problems. When the mind is harnessed properly through intense training, then harmony, understanding and peace will prevail and we can perform great good deeds not only for ourselves, but others also. Let us take an example of a great waterfall. Imagine the great energy that is wasted as the water falls thousands of feet over a high cliff. But when man controls that energy and changes it to electricity, then people benefit from it. But remember, even when the mind is trained, whatever precaution we take to avoid the unsatisfactoriness of our lives, the universal law of impermanence changes everything in this world. This is the nature of existence. Existing things change and disintegrate according to worldly conditions. The combination of elements and energies and their existence together produce objects which we can see and touch, thus giving them an illusion of solidity and permanence. The cause of their change is friction of the elements and energies. When a visible object disintegrates through time it is the dissolution of the elements and energies which have been compounded. The energy is not lost, but goes on into new forms and the process continues without end. This is a natural phenomenon and every component thing is constituted in this way.

There is no reason for us to regard this situation as a certain creation of a supernatural being or that it is the result of punishment for a primordial crime. Buddhists regard this as a natural phenomenon. But many others regard this situation as a problem because changes and impermanence disappoint this craving for permanent existence. The unsatisfactoriness of life begins when we realise that eternity in another life, in heaven or hell, is impossible.

The energies of our bodies are also part of cosmic forces which influence the elements and energies within our physical bodies. Some of our physical and mental problems are due to their influence. Some other unknown forces also disturb our lives which people regard as being caused by evil spirits. Fear, imagination, suspicion and superstition always feed on such beliefs to disturb the mind. When the mind is disturbed, we suffer from physical problems.

However, if our minds are well trained and developed through understanding, we can prevent many of these problems from occurring. That is why the Buddha has said, 'Mind is the fore-runner of all good and evil states, mind made are they.' Actually, we suffer from problems because they are the results of our hallucination. By following the Buddha's advice, we can eradicate fear and ignorance.

How to Face Death

Another problem that people face today is how to come to terms with the death of their loved ones, and this includes parents. We must realize that death is a natural occurrence and however much we love our aged parents we have to realise the biological fact that human cells have a certain life span. A time must come when they stop renewing themselves. It is to be expected that in extreme old age, cells lose their ability to maintain the balance of the destruction and repair process and can no longer maintain the body in a healthy manner.

The history of man is nothing but how he tried to run away from death. Different cultures have tried to run away from death in different ways.

Mind needs a permanent life but life creates an impermanent physical body and we take this as life. After that unsatisfactoriness disturbs the mind.

For those who have lived a long and reasonably happy life and who have strong religious training impending death can even be a welcome phenomenon. When the time comes the dying person becomes composed and leaves the world peacefully, confident that he or she had lived a harmless life and contributed to the progress of man.In societies with deeply entrenched religious beliefs and unadulterated cultural patterns, the concept that death is inevitable and a natural part of the life cycle is accepted. When it does occur in such societies it is treated with philosophic acceptance of the inevitable and is always treated with dignity.

Human beings are the only beings who can understand that one day they will have to face death. That is why they worry unnecessarily about it. Worrying about death will not make it stop, so why not accept it calmly? Shakespeare makes Julius Caesar say:-

> 'Of all the wonders that I yet have
>   heard and seen. It seems to memst
>   strange that men should fear.
> Seeing that death, a necessary end.
>   will come when it will come.'

On the other hand, there are those who do not bother at all about the end of their lives or about what happens after that. However, the majority not only worry about existing problems but also worry about the next life. All other living beings are free from that feeling.

We have to realise that whatever method we adopt to overcome our problems, it is impossible to gain complete satisfaction in our lives until we train our minds and reduce selfish desire. The teachings of the Buddha give us a very clear exposition of how to understand the nature of human problems and how to overcome them and how to face death without fear.

Remember the simple saying in Buddhism, 'Life is uncertain and the death is certain.' Death is not the end of a life. In fact death is the beginning of a life and birth is the beginning of death. The setting sun in this country is the rising sun in another country. Therefore, birth and death are inter-related.

'The birth of a man is the birth of sorrow. The longer he lives the more stupid he becomes. What bitterness. He lives for what is always out of reach. His thirst for survival in the future makes him incapable of living in the present.' *(Chuang Tzu)*

The Buddha reminded us that everything that exists is impermanent. With birth there is death; with arising, there is dissolving; with coming together, there is separation. How can there be birth without death? How can there be arising without dissolving? How can there be coming together without separation?

Birth and death are two ends of the same string. We cannot remove death and leave existence only. First, man struggles to avoid death. After that, he prepares for death. Actually we do not exist but struggle for existence which we call living. ■

THE SANCTITY OF HUMAN LIFE
– Sayings of the Buddha –

Neither for the sake of oneself nor for the sake of another (does a wise person do any wrong); he should not cling to son, wealth, or kingdom (by doing wrong): by unjust means he should not seek his own success. Then (only) such a one is indeed virtuous, wise and righteous. ~84

Though one should live a hundred years, immoral and uncontrolled, yet better, indeed, is a single day's life of one who is moral and contemplative.   ~110

Even an evil-doer sees good as long as evil ripens not; but when it bears fruit, then he sees the evil results.   ~119

Even a good person sees evil so long as good ripens not; but when it bears fruit then the good one sees the good results.   ~120

Whoever harms a harmless person, one pure and guiltless, upon that very fool the evil recoils like fine dust thrown against the wind.
                                                          ~125

Whoever, seeking his own happiness, harms with the rod other pleasure-loving beings experiences no happiness hereafter.   ~*131*

So, when a fool does wrong deeds, he does not realize (their evil nature); by his own deeds the stupid man is tormented, like one burnt by fire.   ~*136*

He who with the rod harms the rodless and harmless, soon will come to one of these states according to his own evil actions:–
     He will be subject to acute pain, disaster, bodily injury, or even grievous sickness, or loss of mind, or oppression, or heavy accusation, or loss of relatives, or destruction of wealth, or ravaging fire. Upon the dissolution of the body such an unwise man will be born in suffering states.   ~*138, 139, 140*

If one holds oneself dear, one should protect oneself well by guarding his mind. During every one of the three watches the wise man should keep vigil.   ~*157*

By oneself, indeed, is evil done; by oneself is one defiled. By oneself is evil left undone; by oneself, indeed, is one purified. Purity and impurity depend on oneself. No one purifies another. ~165

Whoever, by good deed, covers (overcomes, negates) the evil done, such a one illumines this world like the moon freed from clouds. ~173

Ah, happily do we live, without hate amongst the hateful; amidst hateful men we dwell unhating. ~197

Victory breeds hatred. The defeated live in pain. Happily the peaceful live, giving up victory and defeat. ~201

From craving springs grief, from craving springs fear; for him who is wholly free from craving there is no grief, much less fear. ~216

Conquer anger by love. Conquer evil by good. Conquer the stingy by giving. Conquer the liar by truth. ~223

As rust sprung from iron eats itself away when arisen, even so his own deeds lead the transgressor to states of woe. ~240

There is no fire like lust, no grip like hate, no net like delusion, no river like craving.   ~251
Easily seen are others' faults, hard indeed to see are one's own.   Like chaff one winnows others' faults, but one's own (faults) one hides, as a crafty fowler conceals himself by camouflage.
~252

Beings who are ashamed of what is not shameful, and are not ashamed of what is shameful, embrace wrong views, and go to a woeful state.
~316

Beings who see fear in what is not to be feared, and see no fear in the fearsome, embrace false views and go to a woeful state.
~317

Beings knowing wrong as wrong and what is right as right, embrace right views and go to a blissful state.
If you do not get a prudent companion who (is fit) to live with you, who behaves well and is wise, then like a king who leaves a conquered kingdom, you should live alone as an elephant does in the elephant forest.
~329

– The Dhammapada –

With bad advisors forever left behind,
From paths of evil he departs for eternity,
Soon to see the Buddha of Limitless Light
And perfect Samantabhadra's Supreme Vows.

The supreme and endless blessings
of Samantabhadra's deeds,
I now universally transfer.
May every living being, drowning and adrift,
Soon return to the Land of
Limitless Light!

The Vows of Samantabhadra

I vow that when my life approaches its end,
All obstructions will be swept away;
I will see Amitabha Buddha,
And be born in his Land of Ultimate Bliss and Peace.

When reborn in the Western Land,
I will perfect and completely fulfill
Without exception these Great Vows,
To delight and benefit all beings.

The Vows of Samantabhadra
Avatamsaka Sutra

A Path to True Happiness

True Sincerity
toward others
Purity of Mind
within
Equality
in everything we see
Proper Understanding
of ourselves and our environment
Compassion
*by helping others in a wise and
unconditional way*

See Through
to the truth of impermanence
Let Go
of all wandering thoughts and attachments
Freedom
of mind and spirit
Accord With Conditions
go along with the environment
Be Mindful of Buddha Amitabha
*wishing to reach the Pure Land and follow
His Teachings*

NAME OF SPONSOR
助印功德名

47,000 N.T. Dollars:

AMITABHA BUDDHIST SOCIETY OF USA

〔美國淨宗學會〕

1998 Sep., 2000 Copies

以上合計新台幣: **47,000** 元，恭印 **2000** 冊

Document Serial No: 87-054

委印文號: **87-054**

DEDICATION OF MERIT

May the merit and virtues
accrued from this work,
Adorn the Buddha's Pure Land,
Repaying the four kinds
of kindness above,
and relieving the sufferings of
those in the Three Paths below.

May those who see and hear of this,
All bring forth the heart of
Understanding,
And live the Teachings for
the rest of this life,
Then be born together in
The Land of Ultimate Bliss.
Homage to Amitabha Buddha!

NAMO AMITABHA

Reprinted for free distribution by
The Corporate Body of the Buddha Educational Foundation
11 F., 55 Hang Chow South Road Sec 1, Taipei, Taiwan, R.O.C.
Tel: 886-2-23951198 , Fax: 886-2-23913415
Email: overseas@budaedu.org.tw
WWW: http://www.amtb-usa.org
Printed in Taiwan
1998 Sep., 2000 copies
EN083-1381